15 Years in Aphrodite's Fishbowl

A journalist's diary about life in Cyprus, the Island of Love

by

Lucie Robson

The material in this book
was first published by The Cyprus Weekly
between 2008 and 2017.
It is republished here with permission
of The Cyprus Weekly.

For Jean

15 Years in Aphrodite's fishbowl

When I think of Cyprus, whether I am on the island or not, I see its light. At all times of day, the lustrous, radiant, healing, timeless, reassuringly mundane, yet eternal light.

This anthology, though, is a selection of the quotidian.

From 2008 for nine years, I wrote nearly 500 columns for The Cyprus Weekly, an English-language newspaper founded in 1979 which went the way many print publications have gone since the onset of media digitalisation, closing its doors in 2017.

When I started at the paper and was told I had to write a column every week I palled. It's in my nature to keep my views to myself. How can you do either when you have to expose your opinion to thousands of people each week? But, to my surprise, this soon became my favourite part of the job, the task I would leave until after I'd filed my other articles, to slowly savour after all the graft was complete.

I see each column as a tessera, a piece alongside others that, together create a mosaic, an impression of Cyprus.

The columns are arranged, for the most part, chronologically from January to December, in whichever year they were written. There are no chapters, so the book can be read from cover to cover or dipped in and out of.

How did I select a handful of columns from hundreds? Some touch on important events in the island's recent history. Others communicated to me an enduring, essential characteristic about local life over some of the more ephemeral topics.

Why the title? Well, living in Cyprus is a little like living in a fishbowl. Everyone is connected somehow and there's little option for anonymity. And, of course, it's the island of Aphrodite, the goddess of love, so I figured it made sense that it was her fishbowl.

Thanks to the personnel at the Press and Information Office newspaper archives and the Archbishopric Library in Nicosia for their invaluable help in finding some columns I thought I had lost forever. Thanks also to the Fileleftheros Group for permission to reprint the material.

Finally, thanks to Cyprus for its highs, its lows, ups, downs, its brutality, humanity and beauty and above all, its light. The memories of my 15 years on this enigmatic island will remain in my heart for the rest of my life.

January

Nice country…

Over New Year's, I spent a few days in Dubai where people (even the taxi drivers!) say "yes sir, thank you madam, please, have a nice day, have a good evening, we hope you come again and enjoy your flight". In other words, you are treated like a customer.

So, you can imagine my shock arriving back in Cyprus where, in the space of 13 minutes, I was treated like a stable animal, nearly broke my neck on a damp floor and got told off at a newsagent for not having the right change.

"Explain", I hear you say. At passport control, the official in the booth gestured for me to approach in such a way that I had to look behind to make sure that he wasn't signalling to a donkey which happened to be waiting there. But no. There were no animals behind me (not that a donkey should put up with being summoned in such an arrogant, dismissive manner but at least they can stick their hooves in when they're rubbed up the wrong way). I'm a human being so had to hand my passport over. This was checked then flung back at me. (How many times have I had my passport chucked at me in this country?)

Next stop - the washroom…which I couldn't get into because someone had haphazardly abandoned the cleaning cart in such a way that it barricaded the entrance. Being loaded down with bags, I had to shove it aside with the only free extremity I had – a foot – to get inside. Then I nearly slipped on a newly-washed floor which had no warning sign. I sort of sprained my ankle.

Now on to the kiosk. Here I bought two newspapers with a 50-euro note and got berated for it by the cashier. "Am I really being told off at an international airport kiosk in the middle of a trading day for not having the correct change?" I asked myself incredulously as I stuffed my change into my wallet. Yes. I was.

I keep hearing Cyprus tourist authorities banging on and on and on about something called 'Cyprus hospitality' and I really do not know what they are talking about. Does nobody up there have the guts to admit that the emperor has no clothes and recognise that this valuable asset went out with our friend, the donkey? Service levels in the tourist sector are fifty-fifty, hit and miss at best. If you hit, you encounter staff who are examples of professionalism, delivering the kind of courtesy you expect and are entitled to as a customer. If you miss…well…the phrase 'we're doing you a favour' comes to mind.

Welcome back to blinkin' Cyprus I actually grumbled aloud to myself as I limped out of the airport.

Nice country. Shame about the staff.

January 2010

Ideas wanted

I had the most memorable Christmas. I decided to mark the day by attending the ceremonies of three different faiths.

The reason I did this was for the music. I am not religious but admire and appreciate sacred art and thought what better way to enjoy the day than by soaking up the Christmas music of some of the many churches in Paphos? On Christmas Eve, I attended the elegant Anglican service at the beautiful and atmospheric Ayia Kyriaki. On Christmas morning, I got up at 4:30 in the morning to attend the Orthodox service in Moutallos where my Byzantine music teacher is Protopsaltis, or chief cantor. I am lucky to have the privilege of going to services and standing right next to him with other students to follow the music and learn as he sings and chants. This powerful service lasted three rich hours. At noon on Christmas Day, I was back at Ayia Kyriaki to attend the Roman Catholic mass, a heartfelt and joyous service.

I sank into and savoured each because music speaks to everyone whether religious or not.

With Paphos having just received the good news that it's through to the second stage of the European Capital of Culture 2017 bid, it occurred to me that my enjoying a range of religious music was part of what the title is all about. Paphos is now set to compete against the combined efforts of Nicosia and Larnaca in the final months until September, when a special selection committee will make its final decision about the title.

One of the criteria for a successful bid is bringing together the richness and diversity of European cultures in order to foster mutual understanding.

Last year I attended a local festival of Byzantine music which was exceptional. With the town the site of the important part of St. Paul's journey, why not expand such a festival of religious music to incorporate hymns and songs from all faiths, Christian or not? I've also heard that there is a good gospel choir hiding away in Paphos somewhere. It would be nice to hear them come out of the woodwork.

To date, the team behind the bid have kept plans under wraps because of its competitive nature. But, when I interviewed the bid's artistic director, he said that one of the most important team members was the community of Paphos.

So, if you want to see Paphos win the Culture Capital title in 2012 and have suggestions you think could make a difference, keep your ear to the ground about the call for ideas.

January 2012

Clean up your act

I have regrettably had to knock sea swimming on the head this month, not because of the temperature, which is pretty invigorating once you get used to it, but because it is too rough. Still, I go down most afternoons and have a stroll by the sea to get my Mediterranean fix.

The sea itself is always hypnotic but this is spoiled by the litter on the beach. I can't stand it, so my stroll, more often than not, turns into a sort of beach clean-up with me picking up whatever I can and stuffing it into the few and far between tiny trash receptacles (the ones that haven't been knocked down and flattened by a car that is).

Beach clean ups seem to be something of a hobby in Cyprus. I am always bumping into someone who is organising one or taking part in one, promoting one or just undertaking one spontaneously single-handedly. One Swedish resident has even launched an innovative website aimed at promoting a clean Paphos District through inviting the wider community to pinpoint illegal rubbish dumps and kick start a clean-up.

On the one hand I think this is encouraging. It is good to see that the community cares enough about protecting local nature to roll up its sleeves and initiate a tidy up. On the other hand, I think it is disgraceful. I mean where are the local authorities when all of this is going on? Why should I (while taking my seaside walk) and other members of the community find ourselves doubling up as rubbish men when the councils are supposed to take care of cleanliness?

This week, several tourist bodies spoke about the need to get serious about cleaning up Paphos with the start of the Ryanair services come April. Well actually, they have been talking about cleaning up Paphos and creating new green areas for years but, with the launch of weekly year-round services, some of which are serving new destinations, the situation is becoming more critical. It is not enough to bring more desperately-needed tourists to Paphos. They need to like what they see when they get here otherwise it is a wasted opportunity. The new flights are a result of years of negotiation and the implementation of special incentives to attract airlines so, with more perseverance on the part of the local tourist board, more carriers will be coming to Paphos.

Nobody has to look too far to find a revolting pile of trash somewhere it shouldn't be. This is exactly what all of these visitors from new destinations are going to see. With just over two months before the new services start, I would like to see the local authorities campaigning more seriously and less on a superficial PR level to clean up Paphos through encouraging local pride and community action. Most of the new mayors had town and rural cleanliness on their campaign agendas when they were fishing for votes ahead of last December's local polls. It is now time for them to put their money where their mouths are and get creative, innovative and productive in keeping Paphos pristine for tourists and locals alike.

January 2012

If you go down to the woods today

I've always found the recent history of Cyprus' forests an interesting one. The island's forests were in a decimated state round about the time that the British took over the island in 1878. This was a result of centuries of logging for naval vessel building and a plethora of other timber-hungry activities. Under the Ottomans, before the British, a sort of forest taxation was supposed to be introduced with the aim of halting all the wanton tree-felling. But it was never implemented.

In 1879, the year after the British arrived, The Department of Forests was established and since then, through colonial rule, Independence and beyond, the lot of the island's forests improved. The British were very careful about the forests' management and protection. They put an end to uncontrolled goat grazing and introduced protective patrols, reforestation and restoration. In 1951, the Forestry College was set up which, since then, has fed the sector with trained staff.

The forests in Cyprus are magnificent – as all forests are. There is something so uplifting about a healthy forest just like there is something so soul destroying about one which is in bad shape.

This preamble about the island's forests is the backdrop to two pieces of news that caught my eye this week. The first is that illegal lumberjacks are operating to feed a need for wood as an alternative source of heat to expensive electricity. The Forestry Department has detected illegal tree felling and has asked the public to report any incidents and to check the credentials of wood merchants before purchasing logs for heating. How exactly? Do you ask to see a licence before handing over cash for wood or something? And, if so, what does a licence look like? Shouldn't outfits selling wood be obliged to display their credentials/ licence/ rather than putting the onus on consumers to find out what's what? Apart from anything else, demanding to see credentials puts customers in a position of being awkward at best and antagonistic at worst. A little more information please.

The story coincided with one about the new Electricity Authority (EAC) chief promising to try to reduce the cost of power. The EAC has been pretty good during this last financially-difficult year or so with giving customers payment leeway and pledging not to make cuts at critical times etc. But lower power prices? How? The new chief said this was going to happen because of 'radical structural changes' and a 'smooth new phase'. Can someone please translate how this means cuts in power costs?

Unfortunately, I see more pilfering from the forests. You can't blame people. When we are desperate we choose desperate options. Unlike the Ottomans, I just hope that the Forestry Department actually implements its fines.

January 2014

Cyprus what?

It's astonishing how quickly something which has had a presence in daily life for decades can become history in an eye blink.

Two weeks ago, Cyprus Airways was consigned to the rubbish bin after the European Commission ruled that a €65 million aid package issued for 2012 to 2013 breached EU competition laws and the carrier was ordered to repay the amount. Its operating licence was cancelled that same day by the government and, apart from news about protests by former staff about overnight job losses and snippets on the fate of the Cyprus Airways logo, the 68-year-old airline is now a 'was'.

The former national carrier had been on its knees for at least five years with rumours of its demise one week and excitement about potential investment the next. Its drawn out death was becoming painful and I am sure I am not alone in being relieved I don't have to hear about it anymore (although news of more unemployment is never welcome).

Of course, in Paphos, Cyprus Airways died some time ago. Anyone who has lived in the area for a few years will remember how, one by one, the airline ruthlessly plucked its Holland and UK-bound services (amongst others) from the tarmac of Paphos International Airport until the very last route remaining was to Athens. Passengers who used the services routinely were up in arms. The local tourist chiefs were livid especially as they had just spent some time being instrumental in setting up a good bus service linking Limassol passengers with the local airport. "They'd better not," was the sentiment about the possibility that Cyprus Airways would axe its Athens flight as well. But it did, and the spanking new local airport had to carry on minus the national carrier as though Paphos contributed nothing to the economy that contributed to funding the majority state-owned Cyprus Airways. Of course, a similar scenario eventually played out in Larnaca as well. Routes to Tel Aviv, Paris and London's Heathrow were in limbo for a nano-second until Aegean Airlines stepped in like a knight in shining armour to get it all going again.

However, turns out it's a knight in shining armour which doesn't know where Paphos is. I was interested to read Aegean's recent press release about its new raft of routes. "What handy flights are there going to be from Paphos," I wondered to myself. Out of fifteen routes serving Greek cities and major European destinations (Paris – woo-hoo! Milan – hallelujah!) only one, serving Athens, is from Paphos. The rest are between Larnaca and the rest of the world.

On announcing its new routes, Aegean said the following: "With your support, and the efforts of all, our people believe that today marks a new departure for the gradual, but our long-term development of Cyprus."

Sounds good but let's hope that, unlike its predecessor, Aegean knows that Paphos is part of Cyprus.

January 2015

Voter apathy shock

Now the mid-winter silly season is over, I wanted to remark on the trend towards voter abstention in the recent municipal elections.

This is something I never thought I would see in Cyprus. Apathy about politics and voting has been rife in the rest of Europe for years. In contrast to this, one thing that struck me when I came to Cyprus was just how politically-informed and engaged Cypriots were. I was especially surprised at the interest in local politics as I had just come from London where I'd have found it more exciting to watch a darts match in a grimy pub than bother to find out about my local council candidates. I'm not proud of this but it's true. I just didn't care.

Compare this to 2006 when EU citizens were allowed to vote in Cyprus in the municipal polls for the first time; I made darn sure that I got my voting book even though it meant navigating an administrative obstacle course. I intended to put my two cents' worth in because, as a member of a minority, I felt vulnerable. If I didn't make an effort to have my voice heard I'd only have myself to blame.

In Cyprus, yes – much interest in local polls is likely down to the fact that there are vested and personal interests in certain politicians being elected. After all, the smaller a population is, the closer to any centres of administrative power they are and the closer they are, surely the more they are aware of the impact of a vote. This makes the absenteeism at the recent December 18th municipal elections all the more noticeable. By late morning on polling day, the Chief Returning Officer was practically begging people to vote. According to state stats, 37.7% of those registered to vote did not bother – a 9% increase on that of the 2011 elections.

Larnaca was the only district which didn't see a drop in voter turnout. Even in Paphos and Peyia where there were some potentially game-changing contenders, abstention showed a rise.

Although clocked by the authorities, as far as I know, there has not yet been any analysis for this state of affairs. Could it be that the negotiations on the Cyprus Problem, which have been taking place in recent months, were taking centre stage? Were there few candidates to inspire or was it simply, as one of my friends said, politicians promise the earth then forget about it as soon as they are elected? Perhaps it is simply that the call for reform of local government where reduction and merging of municipalities are proposed will make positions more hotly contested, candidates more on the ball and voters care again.

January 2017

It takes a lot of determination to tango

Visiting the UK over the Christmas holidays, my sister and I decided to go to an Argentinian Tango dance night. We have both been doing this dance for several years and one of its beauties is that you can tie an evening of tango into a work or leisure trip just about anywhere in the world. We've danced in vibrant spots like New York, London, Istanbul, and now it appeared we were about to dance in…Stratford St. Andrew (population 185). As a tanguera, you certainly find friends everywhere…

This tiny spot is close to the town where my sister lives in East Anglia. That is, it is close if you don't go back and forth along the A12, veer way off track in the wrong direction and end up having to stop at an outdoor gear shop begging the favour of them bringing up Google Maps on their computer owing to a dearth of road signs. We didn't have Sat Nav, my phone wasn't cooperating and my sister's was on the blink. My sister is a good driver and I have a pretty good sense of direction and can navigate well if the directions match up with the reality (they didn't) and there is the odd sign to indicate where I am heading (there wasn't). But still, what should have been a 20-minute journey max, ended up being more than an hour.

After getting an idea of where we were located and where we should be heading from the helpful gear shop people, we optimistically hit the A12 again in search of a village called Little Glenham (you know how odd English village names can be) through which we had to travel in order to reach our venue. But there was only a sign for a Great Glenham. "Oh, take the turn off," I told my sister desperately. "If there's a Great one, maybe there'll be a Little one nearby."

We quickly veered off and crossed our fingers. It soon became clear that there wasn't anything like a Great Glenham. However, there was a smattering of isolated homes and farm buildings dotted beside a long, long, dark, misty, one-track, tree-overhung English lane, the likes of which I didn't think existed anymore.

This spooky lane went on for what seemed like miles, so we decided we might as well stop for a minute and enjoy the dark, star-studded sky for a bit to calm frayed, exasperated nerves. "I'm determined to find this place," my sister announced after a long silence.

We went on and arrived in the middle of a collection of houses that may or may not have been Stratford St. Andrew (still no signs).

By utter fluke we parked next to what looked like a community centre. "Is that it?" my sister asked. "There are people inside," I said looking. "Hey they're moving". "They're dancing." "They're doing tango." "We've found it!"

The event was fun and the people friendly so the grand tour around the English countryside was worth it in the end. But if you ever feel irked by local directions and lack of pointers, just take a drive in East Anglia. Local signage will seem positively Swiss in comparison.

January 2017

Paphos is reaching new heights

I was struck this week by the comments of Israeli dancer and choreographer, Ido Tadmor, about his participation in the Pafos2017 opening ceremony which takes place on Saturday night. We were talking about his collaboration in the ceremony and, while doing so, he spoke about how he sees the European Culture Capital title that Paphos is holding for the duration of 2017 as a 'rebirth' for the town in dark times. Normally when I do an interview I have a default professional distance from what people tell me, but something about Ido Tadmor's remarks resonated with me personally.

I do think we are living through murky times. Global economic insecurity, horrific terror attacks and political upheaval have not been painting a bright picture. Cyprus has its own 42-and-a-half-year-old weight to carry with the island's division. The recent peace talks, perhaps because they are seen by many as being the last chance for a solution, have set in very clear relief for me just how much energy and focus the national problem has been and continues to take. How many careers have been built around it, how much research has gone into it, how much creativity has it soaked up and how much money has the island's division cost since 1974? Surely a final political decision has to be made and accepted soon in order for the island to move forward.

Against this background, the beacon of Pafos 2017 shines very brightly. It isn't just the achievement of nearly a decade of preparations that even at the best of times, let alone during an economic crisis, would have been challenging to undertake. It is simply so refreshing to see Cyprus, through Paphos' culture title, looking outward and making an impression on the wider stage in an initiative that is not related to UN-brokered talks, the Green Line or the latest political manoeuvrings.

Over the years since Paphos was awarded the culture capital title in 2012, I've come across quite a few friends and acquaintances who have snickered and tittered at the town's win, as though it simply couldn't be capable of pulling off such a major cultural event. I have always had to resist the temptation to smack them. Who says that a place can't reinvent itself and achieve something that seems impossible? Cyprus is so small that what will be good for Paphos can only be good for the rest of the island. It is exciting to see Paphos, through its European Culture Capital title, showing Cyprus what can be possible.

January 2017

All you need is love …
and initiative

During a recent visit to Athens, there was a variety of euros circulating in and out of my wallet. German eagles, Irish Celtic harps, French sowers, ancient Roman generals and Dutch queens mingled, in nickel and brass form, with the archaic Greek owl I'd been given in some change and the Cypriot mouflon I'd flown over with.

And I thought Cyprus was supposed to be a tourist destination.

Let's face it, Cyprus can't compete with its neighbours on the tourist front. It has nothing to touch the splendour of Delphi in Greece, the pyramids in Egypt, Petra in Jordan or Syria's Krak des Chevaliers. Nor Israel's religious legacy, Lebanon's Roman ruins, and Ayia Sofia in Turkey.

Or does it?

Cyprus just might have something that could not only be the envy of the rest of the Eastern Mediterranean but the entire world. This island is the birthplace of Aphrodite, goddess of love – 'l'amour', 'die Liebe', 'amore' and, in Japanese, 'ai'. Now that claim to fame is pretty hard to top.

But, unless I'm missing something, I don't think the Cyprus Tourist Organisation (CTO) has ever really got this.

Naming boxes of sweets and shops after Aphrodite isn't enough. In ancient times, hordes of visitors came from the far reaches of the known world to worship Aphrodite at what is now known as Kouklia. Up the hill from her birth place, Petra tou Romiou, are the haunting remains of her temple and a museum. In Polis, there are her mythical baths and close to Limassol is the temple of her lover, Adonis. In other words, we have the makings of a full-day tour, packed with stories, myths and anecdotes which could be led by an erudite guide.

Instead, there is a do-it-yourself-route booklet hidden amongst all of the other material at the CTO office. And it isn't a case of 'it's better than nothing'. It is not better than nothing. It is absolutely unacceptable that this unique calling card that Cyprus has landed out of pure luck, has never been exploited properly to attract a more diverse range of visitors. The majority of tourists don't go to archaeological remains because they care about the difference between the Mycenaean and Hellenic eras. They go because they are famous. They go because they want to show you a photo and say "look – that's me at Aphrodite's Temple in Cyprus, the Island of Love".

Greece says it's struggling for tourists, but the Acropolis and Delphi seemed pretty crammed to me – with people from all over the world chasing the legends the country is famous for.

The local tourist authorities are currently taking measures to strengthen the tourist product for when the economic crisis passes. I'd advise them not to forget Aphrodite because, I reckon, if she came back to the island today, she wouldn't be impressed. She'd demand that the CTO get its act together or hire a tourism consultant from Athens.

She'd pack her bags and move to Italy. At least there, they have her on their euros.

Date Unknown

February

Safety last

Did anybody notice the construction workers' strike on Tuesday? In Paphos, the scores of half-finished building sites, which appear to have been abandoned because of lack of cash and are starting to look worryingly like remnants from a past age, rang, as usual, with the sounds of silence. And with the state statistics office recently announcing figures which confirmed a slowdown in the construction sector, I can't think of a more inappropriate time for construction workers to strike.

Apparently, more action is on the way if their demands are not addressed. If the sad state of building in Paphos is to continue, this will likely go unnoticed too. The three key points which are irking the labour force in the construction sector are a proposed freeze in the Cost of Living Allowance (CoLA), employment of cheap labour (usually from Eastern Europe and Asia) and the import of sub-contractors brought in from the EU to do tiling and plastering.

Any unionised employee has a right to strike to protect his or her interests and quite a few have been complaining about how CoLA has been getting the freeze treatment across the board. But complaints about EU labour are outrageous. Last time I checked, EU citizens could work legally in another EU state. Cyprus is an EU state. Isn't it?

Also, something that surprises me is the criticism being touted about vis-a-vis the use of what strikers refer to as 'cheap' labour. There has been little 'dialogue' to use the word of the day, about the appalling lack of proper safety conditions for many of these workers. 'Safety Last' could be the catch phrase that would sum up my take on the shabby approach of contractors to safety on the job for their bargain labour.

The most recent state Labour Statistics I could get my hands on said that more than a quarter of fatal and non-fatal labour accidents occur in the construction sector. The Labour Minister pointed out some time ago that Paphos had the worst track record for these incidents. She also stressed that contractors needed to take steps to counter this. I'd like to see a state report on this. Whenever I read about a death or serious injury on a shoddily maintained building site with questionable safety measures in place, it is a Romanian or Bulgarian or Syrian worker who is the victim. It begs one to wonder if they are given the most dangerous jobs and inadequate protection all round.

I was so surprised to see a hard hat on a building site a couple of years back that I was shocked into writing a column about it.

Have any of these indignant striking construction workers considered the risk this non-Cypriot, 'cheap' and oftentimes entirely legal labour faces on the job while slamming their existence for 'undermining' their livelihoods?

February 2012

Charnival!

Am I the only person who had to pause for thought following word that this year's Paphos Carnival King was to be togged up as a Chinese investor?

I am sincerely interested in knowing whose idea this was. And what exactly does a Chinese investor look like anyway? I guess we're going to find out when he enters Paphos on his float to mark the start of the ten-day, pre-lent Carnival festivities.

Traditionally the King, in Paphos at least, has always been a mythological monarch renowned for being loaded, so next week's real-world character is going to be one heck of a turn up for the books. I know that the Carnival parade is meant to reflect local life in some way but let's be honest now; the Paphos Carnival has never been of the ilk of similar parades in Greece where participants go to town on expressing their views on bad state policies through parodic floats and unflattering, brutally honest effigies of terrible leaders. Paphos Carnival has always been extremely tame in comparison. Hence the mythological, wealthy and innocuous King Croesus being hauled out from storage each year to trundle along the streets.

Admittedly, this has changed a bit in recent years. Last year, or the year before last, the Municipality decided to have a more toned-down Carnival King in recognition that the island was starting to enter the direst straits of its economic crisis. But that has been about it. What I'd like to know is, if extremes make one more politically or socially aware, isn't there something else that this year's Carnival King could epitomise other than a fledgling market of investors? What about a figure, mythological or otherwise, drawing attention to the community generosity towards the growing number of people in Paphos who are having a tough time economically? Yes, the whole picture isn't pretty, but it is something to honour and celebrate because, one thing is for sure, the situation is not going to go away overnight.

I mean, when the British were investing locally and making millionaires of Paphians overnight, was there a carnival King created in their honour? Ditto for the Northern Europeans and Russians? I think that if carnival is going to become a means of local expression there are more important things to focus on and express glee about than a handful of investors who will benefit a handful of people.

February 2013

Thank God for the Greens

I know the Green Party can sometimes make you roll your eyes with their picking up on everything from a bit of harmless graffiti on a small patch of wall in an obscure village to ranting about how disruptive to nature an appearance by the Red Arrows is, but there's one thing that makes me want to get down on my knees and kiss the feet of every member of the environmentalist party and that's their relentless demands for animal rights. I'm encouraged that someone out there gives a damn and thinks it's worth ramming down the throats of the public, and the rather indifferent authorities, at every possible opportunity.

There's also Animal Party Cyprus which complements the 'Greens' fervour with facts, figures and a necessary 'cold light of day' approach to promoting the rights of animals.

Thank God also for all the volunteers around the island who contribute what they can to animal welfare and are pretty successful at it as far as I can see (the Tala Monastery Cats, for example, regularly home their charges and The Peyia Private Dog Sanctuary has an impressive rate of homing pets in Cyprus and elsewhere in the EU).

This week the Greens planned a protest outside the Attorney General's Office against the lack of action against lengthening the two-month prison sentence imposed on the barbarian who thought the best way of keeping his dog, Bruno, quiet was by attaching him by his lead to the back of his car and dragging him to death through the streets of Limassol at the end of 2013. I mean who does that? I'll tell you who. The man was reportedly a retired academic. I thought those people were supposed to have some modicum of intelligence.

Likewise, who skins a cat and makes a special effort to string it up a flagpole for all and sundry to see on a Saturday morning in Kouklia? I'll tell you who again. Paphos police told me it was a group of teenagers. So much for educating the young that just because something doesn't walk on two legs it doesn't entitle them to remove its skin or shoot it or lace its food with poison.

I'm not going to quote Gandhi or any other luminaires on this issue, but I will say I don't expect everyone to be an animal lover. However, in my books, if you're an active animal hater and act on this with cruelty, you've got something seriously wrong with you. Remember that man who drove his truck into a man walking his dog near Latchi killing them both because he couldn't stand the sight of an animal near a beach? Do not tell me people like that are normal.

By the way, do you know how long a prison sentence a Neanderthal in South Carolina got last year for dragging his dog behind his car (the dog mercifully survived and was adopted afterwards)? He got five-and-a-half years in prison.

So, thank God for the Greens.

February 2015

Brexit decision time is coming sooner than you think

Was anybody else taken aback at the British PM's recent announcement that a referendum on whether the UK should remain in the EU would take place on June 23 rd this year? Whatever happened to the repeated comments that it was likely to happen no earlier than 2017?

That gave a comfortable amount of time for thorough investigation into what it could mean for British expats living locally.

Do you remember what you were doing around about the end of last October? Well that amount of time from now is when the poll will take place. In my view, this is alarming.

In a nutshell, the focus of the referendum has been immigration, payment of benefits to non-UK EU immigrants and economic autonomy or lack of it – depending on one's perspective and hopes about which way the vote will go. Currently, the percentage of those for and against looks split down the middle.

I have been astonished at the lack of discussion about the impact, if the UK leaves the EU, on day-to-day life. In Britain, how will universities which (increasingly) depend on students from abroad attract anyone from the EU if the fees rise to 'overseas' rates? What happens if you've been paying into the Cyprus pension system for years as an EU citizen and suddenly find yourself stripped of this citizenship? Will UK citizens have to get their passports changed (and bear the cost of doing so) in order to travel? These are just three randomly-picked topics out of countless questions.

Paphos has a high population of British ex-past who could be affected in big and small ways by Brexit. Also, the repercussions for the EU, if the UK leaves could be serious as it would lose one of its largest economies.

If you're a British citizen and want to have a say in the EU referendum, you can vote. Recently, the British High Commission urged people to register to do so.

Mysteriously, this was on the basis that a referendum could be held at any time. Well now it is happening, so if you want to have a say, register. To register as an overseas voter, you must have been registered to vote in the UK in the last 15 years. Once you do register, you can choose how you wish to vote. You can vote by post, by proxy (voting by appointing someone you trust to vote on your behalf), or in person at your UK polling station.

February 2016

Hands off the Cyprus meze

I am all for creativity and experimentation in cooking. But both creativity and experimentation are not benign things in themselves. Using them for their own sakes rather than because they enhance an existing dish is, literally, a recipe for disaster – or at least disgruntled diners.

Let's take the Cyprus meze for example. This is one of My. Favourite. Repasts. Ever.

I'm a vegetarian, so am in heaven as soon as the hot pitta bread and dips sail out of the kitchen. This is followed by a huge village salad to share and small dishes of vegetables, the egg and courgette, the caper leaves, the pickled cauliflower, potatoes in lemon, beetroot, feta, tiganites patates (sounds much better than chips), bourgouri, grilled Halloumi, *kai ta lipa, kai ta lipa, kai ta lipa*. For meat and fish eaters there are additions of loukanika, sheftalia and dolmades as well as little seafood dishes. Everything is fresh. You know what everything is going to taste like. You know how much you are going to manage to eat, so you know how to pace yourself. You start. You halt. You have a glass of wine. You have a chat. You start again. Just when you think you have had enough, out come fresh fruits and shamali cake to finish it off. Somehow you manage these as well.

I am occasionally the kind of diner that a creative chef would adore. I can be in ecstasy about a routine dish that is prepared in a slightly left of-centre way. At the other end of the scale, I am a Plain Jane and don't appreciate certain dishes being messed around with. The Cyprus meze is one of them.

Over the last year, I have had some odd encounters with what was supposed to be the Cyprus meze. I am not by nature a cruel person and I don't believe in dissing people's creativity, be it cultural, managerial or culinary. But let's just say there is no place on the meze table for techni-coloured dips with murky flavours and uniden-tifiable garnishes. There is no place for Halloumi that is cooked in such a way that you need to be told what it is and tastes such that it often returns to the kitchen barely touched. There is also no place for no Halloumi. No meze should be allowed that doesn't have any chips (sorry – tiganites patates) and if there is no egg and courgette I feel cheated. I have no doubt that meat and fish travesties are also appearing on tables across Cyprus.

When chefs start playing with meze in the name of 'gourmet' cooking, I just get grumpy. I end up feeling like a guinea pig and one who is paying for the privilege. If something isn't broken, don't fix it. The Cyprus meze is most certainly not broken.

February 2017

Curb crawling friends

This week I had one of the most unbelievable experiences of my life. I was shamelessly groped in broad daylight.

A little while ago I wrote about how fed up I was with being harassed on the street by seedy, elderly men cruising around in their cars who seem to think they are entitled to honk and yell 'how much?' at you. Well, what happened this week took the golden biscuit.

I was heading home when a car moving in the opposite direction slowed down long enough for its driver to mutter something at me before carrying on. I ignored him and kept on walking, but soon I was aware of a car drifting along directly beside me. It was the same vehicle and this time the driver asked me in Greek if he could 'take me anywhere'. "No, thank you," I replied curtly in Greek and continued. A nanosecond later, I felt a peculiar sweeping sensation from behind. It wasn't until the car passed me completely and I saw the driver's arm and wiggling fingers trailing out of the window that I understood what had happened. The scum bag had reached out and helped himself to a good feel of my posterior, hip and thigh as he slowly drove past (incidentally, as soon as he was past me, he sped up pretty quickly, tearing off down the street and making a sharp right as soon as possible).

If I had had a rock and my wits handy I would have taken a good shot at his back windscreen. But as it was I had neither and was so stunned I just stood with my mouth hanging open, watching the car disappear.

Did I mention this was early afternoon on a main thoroughfare? I had been doing some work in a café so was dressed in roundabout town clothing and carrying my laptop briefcase. In the UK I wouldn't have even attracted a second glance, so what's with the grope-mobile treatment here in Cyprus?

There is definitely a local unwritten law I am unaware of when it comes to these matters. One day you can stroll down a particular street in peace; the next day it's curb crawl city. One particular day of the week is business as usual; the following all of the scuzzes are out trying their luck.

One of my friends has a similar problem when she walks to work at the crack of dawn. She is often harassed by one ancient man or another at 6 am of a morning, for Lord's sake.

I do not think these men would behave the same way if we were Cypriot women. They hear my wonky Greek accent and clock my friend's fair hair and jump to primitive and brainwashed conclusions about how they can address us. I resent this enormously.

February 2017

Coming and going

This week I said goodbye to yet another good friend who has returned to the UK, in this case, for family reasons.

On the surface, I'm used to all of this. How many people with whom I have slowly and carefully developed genuine friendships announce one day that they are packing up and returning to what transpires are their real homes and lives? They leave for a number of reasons. They miss their daughter, or their parents are ill, or they are ill themselves or they are better off financially at home. The list of reasons is endless.

You understand their decision and wish them luck but underneath everything it leaves you feeling hollow. Until you see them again, if you see them again, you will have to keep in touch by email, Skype and the annual Christmas card. I guess we should be grateful for modern technology, but it just isn't the same as meeting up or going out together. Genuine friends are hard to come by anywhere but in Paphos, I have noticed this difficulty has knobs on. For every genuine friend here I have encountered scores of questionable ex-pat characters.

I haven't fared as badly as some people I know. A friend of mine has had experiences with so-called mates that would be at home in a police report. So when you do meet people you like and trust you don't take it for granted. That being said, you get quite good at judging how long someone is going to stick around and, to protect yourself, don't get too close. You become reluctant to invest anything in a friendship because you just know that the person is the type who will up sticks within six months. Nine times out of ten you are right.

This year I already know there are several more people I am going to sadly have to say goodbye to as they leave Cyprus and go home.

It is a strange and disconcerting place where people are forever coming and going.

Date Unknown

March

Take the long road

It has been a long time since I was stranded at the side of the road. Before I got my car, I used to get around on a moped. It was fun during the summer but not during the winter rainy season when the heavens released Niagara Falls.

When I rode my bike, it was the same year that Asprokremnos dam overflowed, which was good for Paphos but not for people who were riding around on mopeds when the engines cut out. Finding myself standing next to my bike at the side of a road in the middle of a typical Cypriot rainstorm is my over-riding memory of that time. I'd stand praying that some kind-hearted person would stop to help me in some way. Preferably he would be a man because (sorry ladies) in my experience a man can magically make anything with wheels go by doing exactly the same thing I unsuccessfully do to it twenty times. The difference is, he does it the first time and it works.

Anyway, I would never be left at the side of the road for long. Soon someone would take pity on me and pull over. More than once, a couple hauled my bike onto the back of their pick-up and drove me first to the mechanic to drop it off, then me on to wherever I had been heading. Considering what I looked like, I'm surprised any-one stopped. With my black, shiny knee-length raincoat, helmet, straggling, soaked hair and protective sunglasses, I wouldn't have stopped for me! But they did.

So, when a few days ago, my car stalled at the side of the road somewhere be-tween Achelia and Yeroskipou where I live, I wasn't worried.

It wasn't my car. My mechanic had done me the favour of lending it to me while mine was in the shop and, to use his words, it 'needed a good service'. Well its luck had run out and as it didn't appear to be MOT'ed, taxed or insured I could forget about a rescue service. Sod's law was in full operation because, out of the three peo-ple who would have been willing to drop what they were doing to help me out, two were out of town and the third wasn't answering his mobile.

So, I got out of the car, crossed the road so as to be facing traffic, and started to walk the four or five kilometres back to Yeroskipou. "I'll be home in 12 minutes," I told myself, "fifteen minutes at the outside. Because someone is going to stop and offer me a lift."

Was I ever wrong! Forty-five minutes later I was still traipsing along the side of the road. This was a country road so there were no pavements and, as I hadn't ex-pected to be rambling that day, I was dressed reasonably smartly, and my high-heels were killing me.

Red-plated rental cars kept whizzing by. This didn't surprise me as their occu-pants probably came from the UK or Germany where they don't stop for anyone at the roadside. But I thought this was Cyprus, so why weren't the dusty pick-up trucks stopping and their drivers saying "Hey kori, do you need any help?" Why were the saloon cars passing without so much as slowing down? Two cars honked at me to let me know they were there but zoomed past. Another got my hopes up when it did a U-turn and headed my way. But it didn't stop.

Weary, a further half hour or so on, I arrived at the edge of Yeroskipou with sore feet and a feeling of disappointment.

People say Cyprus has 'changed'. I never really knew what they meant, but now I do.

March 2009

Parking for beginners

I would like to announce that I am opening a school of motoring with a specialist course in parking lessons for beginners. This is following a frustrating grand tour of the Kato Paphos harbour parking lot, during which I used a quarter tank of petrol in my search for a parking space I could fit into comfortably.

As I chugged around, I'd keep catching a glimpse of a sliver of a space. 'Yippee' I'd say to myself and navigate towards it only to find that, yes, I could just about edge my itsy-bitsy Toyota into it, but it was so tight I wouldn't actually be able to open my door and get out of the car which was pretty pointless as I hadn't driven to the harbour to stare through my windscreen at the herbaceous border lining the lot.

The reason I wouldn't have been able to get out of my car was because of the clutzy, careless way the adjacent car had been parked which meant the vehicle was making incursions into my space. You start to see the wisdom of owning a convertible or at least a car with a sun roof in these situations. You know – things that don't involve having to open doors. True, there are no lines to suggest where the harbour lot parking spaces are. But this really shouldn't be a handicap and, if it is, it's the first thing I will teach you to deal with in my parking school. You just have to mentally measure up and visualise the parking lines which is no more difficult than picturing your shopping list or what you're going to wear that day. You carefully fix the lines in your imagination. Then you confidently steer yourself between the lines. This leaves a roomy gap for the cars on either side.

Some drivers, I have noticed, have problems parking even when there ARE lines marking each space. I can help you with this too. It's really, really easy. You simply manoeuvre your vehicle IN BETWEEN the lines (or maybe I should save this lesson for the advanced course?)

Naturally, I'm not giving away all my training secrets here. You'll learn more if you enrol at my school. You'll learn how to avoid whamming into other parked cars while you reverse out and refresher skills on inventing illegal, ad hoc parking spaces which, at least, leave the road free for other passing vehicles. I'll also teach moped riders how to park in nooks and crannies like they're designed to rather than hogging an entire parking space which a needy car is entitled to instead.

For the launch of my school, I am offering a special rate to those motorists who, I have observed, seem to need the most help in parking considerately. For this reason, I am offering discounts to drivers of pick-up trucks and Mercedes.

March 2011

And now the non-news

On my desk is a piece of paper bearing nine phone numbers, seven for Nicosia and two for Paphos, all surrounded by scribbles of information I have acquired by painstakingly calling each, one after the other, and speaking in my wonky Greek to the people at the other end. In two cases I was transferred internally so let's say eleven phone numbers.

The information I have gathered is that, in order for ex-pats from the EU to get the residency document known as a Yellow Slip, they need to go to their local immigration office and make an appointment. They will be advised which documents to take with them and the charge is €8.54.

No, the police in Nicosia told me, nobody has been arrested to date for not having a Yellow Slip on their person and, if they are from the EU, are highly unlikely to be. Yes, letters are being sent out from The Interior Ministry advising ex-pats that they need the yellow document, Paphos Immigration told me and, 'Nai', officially there is a fine for those who don't possess it but (scratching of the head) they don't know what the sum is. The figure being touted around is €2, 539 but not one person out of the eight I managed to speak to at the police or Immigration could confirm this and nobody answered at the three numbers I was given for Migration. So, I can't say for sure if that figure is correct or under what circumstances such a fine would be issued.

Are you still awake?

Nobody I spoke to in Nicosia and Paphos seemed very well-versed or communicated any urgency on the whole matter suggesting that…it wasn't that important.

The reason I have bothered to write about this at all is that a new storm of confusion about residency documents, much like the Coptic storm we have had in Paphos this week, is billowing around the district. A foggy mucky e-confusion about Yellow Slips, cancelled ID cards and hefty fines is swirling around the web with some half-baked information being circulated from dubious sources (by the way, the first paragraph was to provide an outline of what you have to do if you are a real reporter and not someone who just nicks nebulous third-hand information from another source and disseminates it on the Internet for the purpose of, what I suspect, is profiting from scaremongering – as I have noticed some companies that benefit from providing such 'information' doing).

Certainly, something is going on in the echelons of the Interior Ministry, but it isn't likely to get anyone deported.

Getting a Yellow Slip is straightforward. The procedure is described above. You can go through an agent or you can do it yourself. I did this and now have my

Yellow Slip safely stowed with all my other official docs (I must admit only after I considered framing it owing to the length of time I spent at Immigration sorting it out).

So, if you do go it alone, just make sure you take along enough reading material to the migration office to keep you occupied while you wait. About half the Encyclopaedia-Britannica should do.

March 2012

Nice to know who your friends are

In the worst week in Cyprus' history since the 1974 Turkish invasion, when overnight the public had only limited access to their bank accounts and this only if they happened to have an ATM card and, whatever way you sliced it, the next day, let alone the future was frozen with uncertainty; when British pensioners had their local payments suspended and cash workers couldn't get paid; when nobody knew if there would be any banks operating in the coming week and what would become of their money; when any cash people had managed to secure was being stashed under the proverbial mattress or, in my case, a well-hidden silver evening bag...in the worst week in Cyprus' history since the 1974 Turkish invasion, what did the bakeries do? They tried to help customers' cash go a little bit further by offering freebies of staples with every purchase.

In the worst week in Cyprus' history since the 1974 Turkish invasion, what did the petrol stations do? On the Wednesday they announced they were only accepting cash and no plastic payments because, they said, their suppliers would only take the hard stuff (keeping in mind that at least two petrol station chains supply themselves).

I would have believed this if it had been true. But it didn't appear to be. On Wednesday they were still accepting plastic. On Thursday they were still accepting plastic. On Friday they were still accepting plastic. This was the day the Petrol Station Owners' Association made the dramatic announcement that, as of Saturday, they would only accept cash as though they hadn't been making this dubious statement for three days.

It was beginning to sound a bit like "the banks will reopen tomorrow." In other words, I, for one, wasn't convinced. Even on Saturday morning some were still accepting plastic. And why weren't the petrol stations accepting credit and debit cards anyway? I spoke to JCC on Friday afternoon and plastic transactions were being processed as per normal within one working day. I saw with my own eyes plastic being used on Saturday afternoon at several shops. And who are these suppliers that won't accept anything but cash anyway? I couldn't get any clear answer out of two of the big station chains I contacted. And if there truly was a cash transaction chain going on with a crucial product whether legitimate or not, why didn't a commercial body intervene to pull all parties into line?

I don't care what kind of chaos was looming last week, that was the time to put the foot down and set some standards. Could it have been that the Petrol Station Owners' Association simply wanted to ensure that its members had as much of their customers' dwindling cash supplies (read paragraph one) in the event that things went disastrously pear-shaped on Monday, the day of the EU bailout deadline talks? I call that scare-mongering and profiteering.

In extreme times, you certainly learn who your friends are.

March 2013

Jump on the bandwagon

Today, March 8th, is that, in my opinion, questionable and somewhat patronising civil awareness day, 'International Women's Day'. Still, I am going to refrain from expressing my deepest, most personal views about March 8. All I will say is it irks me that such a day even exists. It irks me so much that I have taken ages to write this week's column and made countless cups of displacement-activity cups of tea to avoid the computer keyboard.

Why does it irk me? Because, in the western world at least, it seems to have turned into nothing more than a convenient day for bandwagon leapers. This week, I have seen it used as an excuse to hold underwear fashion shows in Paphos. I have seen restaurants and cafés encouraging all women to pamper themselves by patronising their establishments while not especially offering anything of a pampering nature. I have even read about the issue of cosmetic surgery vouchers as gifts to the ladies on their 'special day'. Charming.

But even all of these frivolous delights are preferable to the stale calls for 'bridging the salary and status gap' between men and women in the workplace. Are we still talking about this? You know how long Women's Day has been going? For more than a century. And you are seriously telling me we are still talking about this tedious subject?

Well I suppose one look at the new cabinet under new president, Nicos Anastasiades, is one reason (excuse me while I yawn) to see why Women's Day still exists. The new cabinet is all male. Why? I mean, forget discrimination – and when I write discrimination I mean both the usual kind and the equally suspect 'positive' kind. Not having any women in the cabinet is just plain dense in my opinion. Yes, there are two or three seasoned, dynamic and experienced politicians in the new cabinet but, as I read through the list of names, I wondered what was so special about the remaining gentlemen that no women in Cyprus were considered competent enough to be in their position instead. This is written with all due respect to the said gentlemen. Time will tell what mettle they are made of. Just as it would have done for the women who were overlooked for any ministerial positions. So, I guess I'll join in the spirit of the day and wish the Cyprus Cabinet a 'Happy International Women's Day'.

And I have one thing to say to Mr. Anastasiades: shame on you.

March 2013

A Green Monday trek
on snowy Troodos

Green Monday was not so much a day of traditional kites but whites, as a friend and I headed to Troodos for a trek.

My friend has hiked around the Troodos countless times and I've camped there. You'd think we would be prepared for the presence of snow, but we weren't. The forecast looked good. "Don't forget your sunscreen," my friend texted me before leaving. This encouraged me to throw some shorts into my bag. "I'll probably work up a sweat," I told myself, imagining getting a pre-season glow on my skin.

We left at 7am in order to beat the traffic, but the first sign the rest of Cyprus was not planning on joining us was the empty Troodos road. Occasional flashes of snow-peppered mountain tops as we rounded each curve gave us a second sign that maybe it was not trekking season. Still, we arrived at Troodos Square and headed for the trail start which took us a while to locate because the area was covered in a thick layer of icy white stuff that had obviously been there for a while (and was planning to stick around for a bit, too).

Indeed, it was snow. Lots of it.

I have to admit I had never been to the Troodos during the winter before. The part of me that grew up in minus-20-degree, metres-high-snow for-four-months-of-the-year Canada has never really believed that snow in the Mediterranean is real. Yes, there are heavy snow dumps but surely most dissolves under intense sunlight within a few days…doesn't it? My friend, from Sweden, was equally surprised.

We were determined, though, so what followed was a three-and-a-half-hour trek through the seasons, depending on which side of the mountain we were on. On the south side, spring was in the air. On the north side, there was a breath-taking winter wonderland. More than once, one of us took a step and suddenly found ourselves thigh-high in snow. More than once, I had to resist the temptation to slide down a steep, inviting, icy slope. Owing to the snow, we lost the trail a few times, ending up in spots only the Forestry Department has been to, but found it again with the help of a set of footprints and instinct.

By the end we both felt exhilarated, well-exercised, refreshed and a little more in love with Cyprus.

March 2017

April

Christos Anesti

One of my good friends in Paphos, Angelos, is a refugee from the Kyrenia area. Like many people from both sides of the Green Line, he thinks about going back to his village, renamed and repopulated since the 1974 Turkish invasion. But, although he has nearly talked himself into it, he can't bring himself to show his passport at the Green Line to go to his home.

By and by, I've heard quite a lot about his home through stories he's told me, free from sentimentality or bitterness. The simplicity and vividness of his tales have enchanted me.

So, I offered to go to his hillside village with my camera to be his eyes and Angelos agreed. "I don't think you'll find it though," he said. "It's up in the hills and I don't know what it's called now."

He drew me a rough map on a sheet of paper. I decided to go at Easter.

Travelling through and beyond the occupied part of Nicosia, I religiously clocked the landmarks Angelos had drawn because the Turkish names on signposts meant nothing to me. Following the map, I eventually headed off the main stretch up a long, long road filled with crater-like potholes. I worried for the undercarriage of my car. But there was a village nestled on the distant hillside, so I kept going.

When I arrived, dusk was approaching so I got busy with my camera. It was cold, the air smelled of charcoal and nobody was around. I had no way of knowing if it was Angelos' village or not. If it was, according to his map, this little orchard was where he had nicked fruit from his neighbours. That cliff face was where he had hunted baby pigeons with his brother. There was the ancient spring and here was his church, majestically Byzantine.

Then it struck me: it was Easter Saturday, one of the most sacred days in the Orthodox calendar. While churches a few kilometres away on the other side of the Green Line were being prepared for the important evening service, bringing in the words 'Christos Anesti' (Christ has arisen), this one stood morose and silent. The other churches would soon fill with families dressed in their best and holding candles. Fireworks would festoon them at midnight. But this church would stand darkened, empty and uncherished. It hadn't hosted an Easter celebration for three-and-a-half decades and I just chanced to be there to witness it.

I returned to Paphos praying I had the right village caught on my camera. As soon as Angelos shyly but hungrily studied the footage, he confirmed that, indeed, it was his home.

Beneath all the overtures on the political stage, I am often reminded of the silent and tragic human story behind Cyprus' national problem. Thousands of people have had no choice but to accommodate such deep loss into their lives. I don't think there are words to describe how they have managed to do this.

April 2009

Macaroni dinner

I am going to tell you a tale about a man called Joe and some dogs.

Joe is involved in feeding hundreds of dogs. In order to make the cans of dog food go further and provide extra nutrition, it is mixed with pasta. It happens that the dogs' choice of pasta is macaroni. What Joe does is, he cashes in bonus points at different supermarkets for food vouchers to satisfy the dogs' Italian tastes.

The other night, a few of us had collected at Joe's house. We were all chit chatting about what we'd all been up to. Joe's offering went something like this:

It was time to cash in a heap of accrued points for the dogs. He went to a large branch of a supermarket and headed to the customer help desk. He asked the man on duty for some help getting some macaroni together.

"How much would you like," the man asked.

"I'd like €360 worth please," replied Joe.

"Sorry – you – pardon? You want three-hundred-and-sixty…," the flabbergasted man said. Then regaining his professional composure: "Fine. I just need to check the stock."

What followed was the commandeering of all of what was on the supermarket shelves and a good deal of what was behind the scenes.

"How did you get it all to your car," one of us asked. "Well, we needed four trolleys. Three staff members helped." "How did you FIT it all in your car?" "I filled up the boot and the front and back seats. I couldn't see the rear window."

While Joe, an unassuming, elegant and well-spoken man, recounted the tale as though he were repeating the weather forecast he had heard that morning, he didn't understand why we were all nearly rolling around the floor gassing ourselves.

I mean…Joe at the supermarket matter-of-factly clearing out its macaroni stock for the next six years; Joe doggedly (no pun intended) forging ahead across the supermarket parking lot with three staff members dutifully trailing behind, probably privately wondering who his insane Englishman was with his four overloaded trolleys of cut-price macaroni; Joe driving the stash to the dogs, unable to see anything because his vehicle was packed to the hilt with bags of macaroni cascading everywhere whenever he hit a roundabout or a sharp bend (I couldn't shake this image even after Joe told me the macaroni had all been safely boxed up).

I'm not making fun of Joe. I told him I'd write about his mission because it is important to publicise what it was for. He was cashing in bonus points for the Paphiakos and CCP Animal Welfare food scheme for the scores of animals at its shelter. Many people want to help an animal charity but don't have the time. One way of providing some very important help is by donating supermarket points. As Joe's account demonstrates, the points add up and make a difference. Please just have mercy on the Italian food lovers and don't clear out the pasta section.

April 2012

Leeway

We learned this week that state coffers were boosted by €19 mln courtesy of a segment of corporate tax, the new annual €350 levy on registered companies aimed at helping to put the economy to rights. So far one fifth of the 250, 000 companies on the register have coughed up what, for some, is a negligible amount but, for small enterprises in particular, another burdensome expense in tight times.

I have already written realms about how small to medium-sized enterprises (SMEs) are struggling to balance their books. Clients, who are also balancing their books, are paying late or not at all. Staff still have to be paid, although it is no secret that many are remunerated late on a routine basis because of aforementioned late paying clients.

C'est la vie. 2012 is going to be a tough year for all tax payers with VAT rising along with an increase in social security payments to name two of the measures in the austerity package which has been pushed through the House of Representatives. The island's back is against the wall and nobody, except some civil servants who think they are living in a parallel universe where euros grow on trees amongst the lemons and oranges, is entitled to be exempt from doing their bolstering bit.

Amidst all of this, the banks and VAT office won't wait for anyone.

I have many friends and colleagues in Paphos who run SMEs and they are fed up with being given little leeway by the banks on loan repayments and no leeway whatsoever by the VAT office on their tax payment schedule.

One of my struggling friends was fined by VAT for paying a day late – something in all her years of business she had never done. The reason she paid a day late was she only had part of the money owed. The reason she had only part of the money owed was because, although she had carefully banked VAT payments as they came in, late-paying clients meant she had to dip into some of this money to cover other imminent responsibilities which also won't wait for anyone. If the VAT office had given her five day's leeway, she would have been able to scrape together the remaining sum. I have many similar bank fee-related stories, but let's not go there.

SMEs are the backbone of Cyprus' economy. According to the most recent EU figures, they constitute 99.8% of operating companies. The figure of 83% of jobs provided by SMEs is one of the highest of all EU-27 and the average number of people working for each is slightly higher than the EU average.

Perhaps tax, tax and more tax is not going to bring SMEs to their knees but a lack of leeway, I have little doubt from what I have seen in my circle, could do so, bringing their above EU average number of employees down with them.

Banks and, of course, the VAT office ultimately take their operational cues from state legislation. Maybe it is about time that the government, while demanding more cash simultaneously gave SMEs a little more slack to help them meet their relentless financial obligations.

These enterprises can't bring airports to their knees and bugger up people's travel plans through hissy fit, knee-jerk reaction type strikes of the type we have seen recently. Neither can they interfere with the democratic process of voting by threatening to stay at home on polling day, both recent antics of public sector unions. But they employ 83% of the workforce. That should be reason enough for the government to start ensuring they are taken care of.

April 2012

On the buses

Interesting to hear that some of the island bus companies have noticed a rise in the use of public transport this year. They put it down to the 'living-on-a-shoe-string' situation that many people are facing and suggest a "small rise" in the €1 ticket price in order to upgrade the service all round to make it even more attractive. The increase will make riding the bus "a pleasant experience" they say and put a better service in place for when the economy is back on track, therefore making it a long-term option.

I'm still not sure if this is just being seen as a chance to make a quick buck or a sincere idea. The buses are brand new and already look pretty pleasant to travel on, but I do agree with the bus companies that the service needs upgrading. Specifically, they need to run more frequently to be able to accommodate people who want to use them for work. Plus, they need to run later and earlier.

I've travelled on the inter-city buses a few times. The only complaint I have about them is that they don't have toilets - and I bet there is an EU law against that. But the bus company's assumption that bus travel is unattractive sums up a snobby attitude towards public transport in Cyprus which needs to be chucked out in light of the financial meltdown the island is going through.

I have to own a car because I have to get around and about for my job at irregular times. But, with due respect to my little vehicle, I would choose a good public transport any day of the week over car ownership. I can't see that the latter is anything but an utter waste of money, resources and inefficient all round.

The two public transport systems that I have the most personal experience with are the ones in London and Toronto. Just to enlighten anyone who sees travelling on public transport as beneath them, I can assure you that people who ride on buses and other forms of public transport do wash themselves. Also, many of them, in the aforementioned cities even have high-flying, well-paid jobs and, in spite of this, have no objection to lining up for a bus or underground train and riding with all the 'riff-raff'.

Maybe some of our politicians should set an example and use the buses from time-to-time to help dislodge the local stigma attached to it. Remember how former London Mayor Ken Livingstone famously rode in the underground every day to work?

April 2014

The history of the Ouzini

I have to hand it to one Dr. Michael Paraskos of Lemba for his creation of a new national cocktail for Cyprus, especially as I personally see nothing wrong with the traditional, divine, refreshing and any-time-after-three-in-the afternoon blend of brandy, soda, lemon squash and Angostura bitters which is the Cypriot Brandy Sour. I certainly do not agree with his description of the Brandy Sour as "tired" and "old" (unless you have it in certain Paphos hotel bars which shall remain nameless).

Still, creativity on any front is always welcome, so I was interested in reading about this new drink which was made in response to a Cyprus Tourism Organisation call for inventiveness with local ingredients and promotion of Cypriot cuisine.

The Ouzini is made of one-part Ouzo, three parts freshly-squeezed orange juice and two to four drops of Cyprus Bitters. I always thought that ouzo was Greek but, as I'm fond of this spirit and the recipe calls for 'Cyprus Ouzo', I'll let that one go. You mix it all in a long glass over ice and it's ready to sip. Sounds like it's worth a try.

Now all we need is a vintage story to go with the cocktail. Most of you probably know the tale of the Brandy Sour. Legend has it that it was created for King Farouk of Egypt who was a regular visitor to the Forest Park Hotel in Platres. The king liked a tipple but could not be seen drinking alcohol because of his Islamic faith. To make life as pleasant as possible for their guest, the hotel management came up with an ingenious form of "iced tea" which could be drunk in public. It was, of course, the Brandy Sour.

I think this is a pretty classy story for a cocktail.

It's worth noting however, that the Ouzini is not the first cocktail which has aimed at usurping the Brandy Sour. A few years ago, a teenager created a drink called the "Fire and Forget" which won the pan-Cyprian Original Cyprus Cocktail Competition. It was a combination of Ouzo, Zivania, Nama sweet dessert wine, orange liqueur, pomegranate, orange juice and a touch of rose cordial. It also sounds quite tempting, but I don't think I have heard of it since.

Which goes to show it's possible that to endure, a cocktail needs a tale.

April 2016

Enabling the disabled through the Cyprus plan

While the current drafting of a Council of Europe Strategy on Disability National Action Plan announced in recent days looks good on paper, it is daily practicalities I have a problem with. Under this European initiative, people with disabilities are defined as "those who have long-term physical, mental, intellectual, or sensory impairments which, in interaction with various barriers, may hinder their full and effective participation in society on an equal basis with others".

The objective is to tackle this on eight fronts: Accessibility, Education, Employment and Training, Participation, Education, Social Protection, Health and External Action. I would add two more points; the privilege of being able to use the restroom in a restaurant you have just patronised and that of moving along a pavement unhindered.

Time and time again, I see neither of these needs being respected. The National Action Plan for Disability (2017-2020), as it is officially known, is only one strand of activity aimed at improving the lives of people with physical disabilities. It is necessary but cannot resolve all the issues faced by such people, as defined above. For instance, if drivers continue to park their cars on pavements in a willy-nilly manner that blocks a pedestrian's path, I can't see that the National Action Plan for Disability is going to be very effective. Sometimes, if I'm carrying a few bags, I'm retarded on my path along a pavement because a vehicle occupies the middle of it. I can just about get by it if I either raise my shopping above my waist and walk sideways or step into the road. Anyone in a wheelchair or using a walker can forget it. They must wait until the selfish driver reappears.

And how many Paphos toilets are simply inaccessible? What must it be like to have limited mobility and to have spent money in a bar or restaurant to find that to reach the washroom you need to go up one of those precarious winding metal staircases that Paphos is full of? Even I tread carefully on those and I'm (touch wood) able-bodied.

I don't know how some of these venues pass tourism and planning criteria. If the police don't start getting tough on illegal parking and venues can carry on plonking their toilet wherever it suits them, the National Action Plan for Disability will, ultimately, not be worth the paper it is printed on.

April 2017

May

Who needs Hyde Park corner?

In my diary for this weekend, Kataklysmos, there is a thick, black line across "Red Arrows! Yippee!!!"

I buy environmentally-friendly cleaning products, recycle and walk where I can; but I was looking forward to the cancelled RAF Red Arrows aerobatic show. Is that all right?

This question is directed at the Green Party which appears to be the holier-than-thou Red Arrows party-poopers. "It ignores the environmental damage, noise and risks that the show will cause," the Greens said in a release that struck me as being a cross between a Greek drama and Soviet politburo speech. "It is a silly event of the colonisers," they went on – and "Paphos Municipality is selling the dignity of the people of Paphos for a few euros."

Oh, lighten up why don't you, Green Party? We're talking about a one-off event which could have given Paphos tourism a shot in its weakening arm. The Red Arrows are no more disturbing than a scenic herd of agritourism goats clattering across the road or the sound of recycling bins being emptied at four o'clock in the morning (which is what happens in my neighbourhood).

OK – I can accept that it is your job to make a stance about anything that adds to the ozone hole (and thank goodness somebody is). But what's this blinking 'colonialist' business? Who needs Hyde Park Corner when you've got plenty of this kind of off-key ranting here in Cyprus?

If any readers aren't familiar with Hyde Park Corner, you have to go there one day. It's a spot in London were any lunatic can go and air treasured racist, bigoted, sexist, wonky, weird and occasionally, intelligent opinions. I can easily see the Green party there with their anachronistic, xenophobic 'saving the dignity of the Paphos people against the colonialists' stance. I mean, please tell me if I have got something wrong here, but didn't the British leave Cyprus half a century ago? I'm gobsmacked that the word 'colonialist' is still alive and well in the local vocabulary let alone thriving in full sentences like 'silly colonialist games'. Wouldn't the EOKA freedom fighters be stunned too? And what remarks to come from the Green Party who always claim to be so right on, progressive and 21st century? I gave them more credit.

Paphos Municipality say they cancelled the show because of the threat of a Green Party demo. They're scared of THAT? Have you ever been to a Green Party demonstration? You've probably walked right through one without noticing. With due respect to you environmentalists, you must admit yourselves that they aren't the most populated, raucous events. And since when does the municipality listen to the Greens? The last time I checked they couldn't stand one another.

Never mind. This Kataklysmos weekend we'll no doubt have the usual Cypriot

folkloric music and dance troupe entertaining in the harbour instead. If we're lucky,
. they'll treat us to a re-enaction of a traditional wedding like they do every year.
That's bound to draw a crowd from all corners of Cyprus.

May 2010

Where was the tumbleweed?

The only thing missing from the desolate scene in Paphos Harbour on Kataklysmos Sunday last weekend was the tumbleweed.

I wandered down there with a friend and found a parking spot with ease. If we had wanted to, we could have played Blind Man's Bluff from one end of the harbour promenade to the other without touching anyone. Why? Because the cafés were half empty. This on a long weekend holiday in May.

Of the customers who were there, I can't say they looked particularly jubilant about having been saved from the clutches of Colonialist Humiliation.

What IS she on about, you may be thinking? Does the date May 23, last Sunday, ring a bell with you? You know…the day the RAF aerobatic team, the Red Arrows, were supposed to perform in Paphos Harbour but which got axed because the Green Party said that the air show was a silly colonialist display that would 'Compromise the Dignity of the People of Paphos'? Forgetting that half of Paphos is made up of foreigners, who conveniently become invisible when this matter of colonialist paranoia rears its head.

Paphos Municipality, which normally detest the Green Party, for some reason, listened to them, so retracted the licence for the show.

I have spent all my spleen about the silly reasons for cancelling what could have been a money-making event in a previous Paphos Notes and am too weary to vent it all again. But I will say that you can't put my disgust at the cancellation down to me being British. I appreciate the culture I come from, but I have few drops of patriotic blood in my body. The appearance of red, white and blue, the colours the Red Arrows emit during their shows does nothing for me. Neither am I huge fan of air shows, so you can't say I am a biased fanatic. But I am a fan of seeing Paphos harbour heaving on a holiday weekend in May like it should be. I reckon that the businesses down there would feel the same way.

The panagyri traders lining the sea hawking toys, sweets and CDs, didn't even cover their costs this year. Clearly the donkey rides were not enough of a pull. The presence of an attraction like The Red Arrows could have made a difference.

May 2010

Shades of green

One of the local authorities which shall, for the time being at least, remain nameless, has decided that it suddenly cares deeply about Green Areas and land distribution quotas around apartment buildings hidden in the back streets of its precinct. It has decided that the postage stamp-sized area adjacent to my friend's apartment building is in need of a special makeover so that it falls in line with a Green Area ratio dictated by law.

To this end, it is going dig up four mature banana trees, an apricot tree, two decorative shrubs and any seeds which have been planted by my friend. You see, for several years, my friend has been growing vegetables, as a hobby, on this tiny, hitherto 'uncared-about-and-unnoticed-by-the-municipality' piece of land. In place of the vegetable garden, the local authorities are going to lay a decorative garden in order to fulfil their Green Areas quotient. This garden will have a scattering of olive trees planted in tightly-packed earth.

So, this will mean the end to the bags of aubergines, courgettes, red cabbages, green peppers, etc, etc, that my friend has dished out to his neighbours from his thriving garden over the years.

I don't know…I thought that things like banana trees, shrubs and leaves on aubergine plants WERE green.

In normal times this wouldn't annoy me so much. I am used to the authorities in Cyprus suddenly and illogically deciding to abide by the letter of the law when it suits them. But this happens to be one of the Paphos local authorities which is taking on an initiative to develop community vegetable gardens to help the growing number of people who are struggling because of the financial crisis. Details of the plan are being finalised, but the gist of the project is that a select group of people will learn how to cultivate vegetables and then reap the bounty. Any excess can be sold.

It sounds rather like what my friend has been doing quietly off his own back for years – minus the selling bit. I bet this year the neighbours in my friend's apartment building need those aubergines and courgettes more than ever. So why don't you red-tape bureaucrats quit being so flipping anal and back off?

May 2013

Let it rain

I have developed a special way of washing up. I will put everything in the empty sink and douse it in water. Then I will spurt the washing up liquid all over it. Next, I pick up each item and scrub it to within an inch of its life, getting it all soaped up. After this I replace it in the empty sink until all of the items have been scrubbed and sudded thoroughly. Finally, I will rinse everything carefully and place each item on the draining board. It's kind of like I am camping and have limited water stores.

Apparently, the lack of rain this winter means that we could be in for the toughest year water supply-wise since 1901. Well forget about 1901. I was alive in 2008 and remember the way of washing up I just described was one of the water-saving tips which was encouraged, along with turning off the tap while brushing your teeth instead of leaving it running and more or less doing the same when you are having a shower. These habits became so ingrained six years ago that I still carry them out nearly every day today.

The winter has been so dry and the dams are not even 50% full. Has anyone else forgotten some of the 2008 drought fiascos? Some neighbourhoods had no water while other did (mine did which is probably why I guiltily saved water). I don't recall that one person was charged for obnoxiously hosing down their porches and gardens twice a day even though it carried a fine. Water-carrying ships from Greece were stranded by just sufficient metres offshore to trigger some ridiculous cock up over urgent water distribution to the worst-hit areas.

Who wants any of this again? I personally want a few more spring showers. Either that, or I sincerely hope that the authorities in question are prepared this time for the drought many project is coming this summer.

May 2014

Carry on constable

Ever since a high-ranking Paphos police officer winked at me at a press conference, I have had my doubts about the local police force. It wasn't a lecherous wink. It was an innocent, paternal, 'how are you today young lady' sort of wink like what my dad used to give me when I was a little girl. But I am not a little girl and this policeman, who shall remain nameless, was not my dad.

The Paphos police force is tottering perilously on the brink of looking like a Carry-On film. If you aren't familiar with the British Carry On series, think parody, double entendres, slapstick humour and dumb blondes (and brunettes, and red heads…). I mean in the space of one week, we had what felt like an abdication of the Police Chief (he didn't even say goodbye), his successor digging his heels in and resigning over being assigned to 'backwater' Paphos, two terrible murders – one which was possibly caused by an appalling delay in police response, and a serious case of one officer sticking his hand in the till. I keep expecting Carry On actors Barbara Windsor and Sid James to turn up.

Oh – and I didn't mention that in the same week there was a little public relations announcement about a police guard who apprehended a criminal while the latter tried to escape from Paphos General Hospital, where he was a patient. The guard chased the would-be escapee from the third-floor window to the second floor where he nabbed him, and it seems there is going to be an honouring ceremony from him next month. Well, good for him but, a) he was just doing his job and b) don't forget that the hospital is pyramid-shaped, so you don't have to be Spiderman to climb from floor to floor. I'm afraid it will take more than trumpeting about this kind of action to bolster ailing confidence in the Paphos police.

London, with a population of about 7.5 million people had 156 homicides last year. The figure for Paphos, with a figure of 75, 000, was 5 (and I had to trawl through my own records for this because, disappointingly, I got no help from Paphos Police press office). Put another way, there is a 0.0002% change of falling victim to a murder in London. In Paphos, the percentage rises to 0.007%. I am not suggesting that Paphos is as dangerous as a large metropolis. But I think the figures show that we are not living in such a safe and sleepy little district anymore.

The new Chief of Police posted at the start of the week has his work cut out for him. He seems to be determined to cooperate with local police to increase security and clampdown on crime and corruption within the force. Let's hope, for all our sakes, that he irons out the kinks in Paphos police operations because I'd hate to see him land the starring role in 'Carry on Constable'.

Date unknown

June

Summer nights

When I first arrived in Cyprus it was spring, and the UK ex-pats immediately started to warn me about the 'horrors' of the approaching summer heat. Privately, I thought 'what a bunch of wimpy Brits'. The British just don't 'do' weather extremes. Two-and-a-half centimetres of snow land in London and the trains stop.

Because I spent most of my school years in Canada, where in summer you can forget about sleep if you don't have A/C and milk curdles just carrying it for six minutes from the shop to home, I listened patiently to the warnings that "you must get everything done by 9am and put loads of water out for the stray cats or they'll dehydrate and be prepared to get no sleep until October". "Yeah, yeah," I thought.

But, by early June, I discovered I was a 'wimpy' Brit myself. By 8am the heat was so oppressive I felt as though I was sitting in an open-air sauna. At night, I often set up a makeshift bed on the balcony in the hopes of getting a scrap of breeze and two hours' sleep. These days, years on, I stock up on electrolytes and still groan about the heat along with everyone else, but only half-heartedly, because I have grown to love summer in Paphos.

It isn't just the lush greenery, the way the Mediterranean changes colour and the syrupy light. It is all the culture that explodes in every corner of Paphos district. I don't know how anyone can say that there is nothing to do in Paphos in the summer. Tonight, the high-standard annual Pancyprian choir festival takes place at the atmospheric Ancient Odeon in Kato Paphos. Next week, the annual Ancient Greek Drama Festival starts at the same venue – which, by the way, is where the Romans watched their theatre millennia ago. It doesn't even matter if you don't understand the language because knowledge of the story is enough to enjoy productions like Medea, Antigone and Elektra. A few days ago, I went to 'Eis Aphrodite', a concert of music by Mikis Theodorakis, which took place right in the middle of Aphrodite's temple precinct. It was impeccably organised by the Yeroskipou and Kouklia municipalities and the singers and musicians were excellent. I even enjoyed 'Zorba the Greek', a piece of music I thought I hated having seen too many half-cut tourists trying to dance to it in tavernas. Last Sunday, World Music Day was held in Castle Square which saw local and Greek acts, including Dimitra Galania, performing – and all for free. In August there will be a medley of live jazz at the truly heavenly Paradise Place in Pomos and in September, the opera, Lakmé, will be performed under the stars at Paphos harbour.

I already know that, if I ever leave Cyprus, these sultry summer nights are the things I will miss and, from time to time, long for.

June 2009

A happy ending

I was lucky to be privy to a happy ending last week when three beautiful leopards flew out of Paphos Airport to a life of freedom.

The leopards were released from cramped conditions at Limassol zoo through the persistent pressure of the Born Free Foundation along with local animal activist groups and sent to South Africa to live out their days on a reserve.

What is it about the magic of animals? When the leopards arrived from Limassol, ground staff got busy unbuckling this and loading up that and the police strutted about officiously. But you could tell that everyone was in awe. The police examined the containers with their torches, revealing black and golden spotted coats and whiskered muzzles. They let the beams linger a little longer than they needed to so, I suspect, they could soak up the sight.

Ground staff had their mobile phones out for quick shots in between stamping the containers. The best bit for me was when the leopards were on the tarmac about to be boarded into the aircraft hold and a photo shoot was set up. Their handler removed the wooden hoarding from the front of a cage to reveal one of the regal creatures. Airline staff lined up next to the box and smiled. The media flapped around. But the leopard just lay curled with its chin on its folded paws, cool as a cucumber, gazing out at the humans and blinking in that lazy feline way as cameras flashed around it.

Every time a picture was taken, its eyes glowed in reflection, but it stayed perfectly still. Then the hoarding was down, and the show was over.

The following day, whenever I heard a plane overhead, I thought of the leopards dozing in the hold of an aircraft on their long journey to their new lives.

It's heartening, from time to time, to cover a story with a happy ending.

June 2009

Grace

On the way to covering the Pope's arrival in Paphos last week, three Syrians happened to complain to me that the roads all had police blocks and asked me if I knew why.

"The Pope is coming from Rome," I told them.

"Oh," they said.

A few days earlier, an Orthodox friend had told me the visit meant little to him either.

I was pretty much in the same boat because I'm not religious. The Pope's visit was just another news story. This made the scene at Ayia Kyriaki in Kato Paphos, where the Pontiff would make an address, seem especially surreal.

Hordes of worshippers had congregated and were singing, dancing and even hollering in football match fashion about Pope Benedict XVI.

While the crowds expressed joy, wonder and exuberance, I clinically cast my eye about from the media section and did the usual mental inventory of what to include in a report.

Then the international press corps arrives (all impeccably dressed in black) and positioned themselves in their allocated area right in front of the crowd.

Their arrival mean that the Pope was coming soon so the worshippers, whose view was now blocked, got angry. This all went into my mental notebook.

All the while, a police surveillance helicopter circled noisily overhead, the heat melted down on us and dust hung in the air.

The Pope came, spoke eloquently, and departed and everyone seemed satisfied in the end.

But, what had possibly been the most important day of those worshippers' lives, had just been another report for me. I felt inexplicably jaded and weary driving home.

Later, though, a memory surfaced.

Last year, when my father lay literally about to die of pancreatic cancer in Toronto, a Catholic priest prayed for him.

I wasn't at the hospital because I was still in Cyprus. My family told me. They hadn't been there either because no night visitors were allowed, and it had happened first thing in the morning. The Catholic priest had, in turn told them.

My father was in the heart ward by fluke because there was no room in palliative care. The priest had been transferred to the adjacent bed after cardiac surgery. He was woken the next morning by medics frantically flapping around my father's bed. The priest understood what was happening and immediately started praying for my father.

I personally find organised religion baffling, but I understood and will always be grateful the priest's gesture. Isn't the kind of generosity he showed, what any faith is essentially about?

June 2010

Ice cream arithmetic

My friend and I went to a punishing session at the gym for two hours then went sea swimming then attended a gruelling Pilates class. After this, we felt we were entitled to multiple scoops of ice cream.

I am lying. We didn't engage in any of this exercise. However, we did take a long evening walk along the Pharos Beach in Kato Paphos which led to the Paphos Harbour promenade where we counted seven ice cream shops in the space of about 500 metres. So perhaps we hadn't shed gazillions of calories but this long seaside walk plus the pressures of daily life in Cyprus these days made us gravitate towards said ice cream shops.

At the end of the Pharos walk we both immediately fell into a strategically-located ice cream parlour where my friend bought a one-scoop chocolate cone. This lasted out past all the cafés, a bogus fortune telling machine which took our money and gave us no predictions and the walk past the car park until we hit the promenade proper.

Here I decided I had an ice cream craving. My friend, who had only just finished her chocolate affair, decided she did too. So, we fell into another parlour, sampled a few flavours, then each got chocolate varieties which were such stingy servings that they got lost in the cone. Even the additional glob of hazelnut sauce my friend ordered didn't bring the contents up to the rim of her cone. Still, she generously let me appropriate some.

But so unsatisfying was this measly-sized ice cream that, as soon as I had finished mine I declared I wanted another. Luckily another ice cream parlour loomed ahead. My friend ordered a double scoop of caramel and chocolate and I ordered a single scoop of the latter. Waiting to have our cones bestowed on us we already knew we had hit the jackpot. The assistant made a few jokes as she tried to scrape the rock-hard ice cream out with the scoop and it was evident that they were going to be large ones. They also happened to be the cheapest. And the best.

The point of this indulgent tale is that we were stunned at the difference in price range (from €1.20 per scoop to €2), quality and the quantities we were served all along the same tourist stretch. Don't these parlours check out the competition? And don't they think anyone notices?

Speaking of competition, there are four more ice cream joints we didn't investigate. We'll get back to you about them.

June 2013

Summer woes

You know that summer has arrived in Paphos when, along the seafront promenade topless beer-bellied men, perspiring in the heat, quiver along apparently oblivious to how much they are disgusting passers-by. I say 'apparently' because I don't think for a minute that they are oblivious. I think the complacent attitude is "I am coming to your country and putting cash in your coffers, so I can walk around looking like a grub and you can like it or lump it". Well actually I think I'll retch and vomit instead if you don't mind.

Yes, Cyprus is a hot country, but have you ever heard of cotton? You'll be a little warmer in a good cotton shirt and spare everyone else the repulsive sight of your tattooed mega stomach wobbling along with sweat dripping off it.

I am not being flippantly facetious about people with weight problems either. But I don't think these beer-bellied stunners fall into that category. It is simpler than that. They have just let themselves go and think everyone else should put up with looking at them.

In the privacy of my home when the heat is unbearable, and I am alone, I throw on tacky little none-outfits just to keep cool. But I would never subject anyone on the street to my anti-heat home look. To me, this flabby tourist look is just arrogant and typical of the crummy standards of the day. It is also unhygienic. These guys park themselves in bars, cafés and restaurants and their sweaty, flabby torsos rub against the seats that other people will use later.

It is also off-putting. I would lose my appetite if I had to share a restaurant with one of these topless lovelies. Many local entertainment spots and supermarkets feebly and futilely indicate that they expect customers to dress with some modicum of modesty through signs and notices at their entrances. Judging from the clientele, they are not heeded, and you can't blame proprietors for putting up with it all. It's money.

On the beach or at beach bar it is fine but everywhere else? What can be done to make this variety of tourist show some respect – because that is most certainly what is lacking.

June 2013

What will it take?

The Interior Minister has admitted recently that the state has 'failed miserably' on issuing title deeds, a stipulation of international lenders and with a serious deadline at the end of this year. By the close of 2014, the government is meant to bring the number of outstanding deeds down to a maximum of about 2, 000. If it doesn't, it may risk losing the next tranche of aid which is part of the bailout terms triggered by the banking crisis in March 2013.

Presently, there are approximately 28,000 outstanding title deeds. The Interior Minister, addressing the House Watchdog Committee said that the economy of Cyprus was under threat if it did not take action over the matter. Pressure groups on title deeds have been saying the same thing for years. At least the minister had the grace to make a sort of admission of failure (although I am extremely suspicious as to why politicians choose to say anything that comes out of their mouths). But let's give him a little pat on the back for saying such a thing - especially as the problem pre-dates the present administration. And the one before come to think of it. Yes. The title deeds saga goes back a very long way. I am having trouble stifling a big fat yawn at the moment about it.

It is not that I regard the matter flippantly. Far from it. To the contrary, the yawn is being generated by the demi-meaningless words that have been uttered by successive politicians over the years. I mean, how is the state going to clear a backlog of 28,000 deeds within the remaining five-and-a-half months of the year? It has barely made a dent in the mountain of deeds in the last five-and-a half years! Yes, it started to tackle the issue under the last administration, but it has been slow work.

I think of all of the pressure put on the relevant authorities over the years by action groups which were more than willing to cooperate in order to cause minimal damage to Cyprus' reputation as a place for property investment. Why would the action groups have wanted to damage the island's reputation? They had and have an interest in the island having a good reputation on the property front. But still, the government and parliament didn't pay much attention until the foreign, mostly British media, picked up on the story and ran reports and broadcast programmes about the dangers of investing in the local property market. Then, all of a sudden, the action groups were trying to "sabotage" the property sector.

The media is always looking for stories and with the communication available today, it was only a matter of time before news outfits beyond local shores picked up on it all. Well, maybe if the state had paid some serious attention to the pleas of groups and individuals calling for the release of deeds, the foreign media wouldn't have had so much to sink their teeth into.

The minister also spoke of the financial sense it made to release deeds referring to the potential hundreds of millions of euros it would release into state coffers through transfer deeds. The action groups brought this up with the government time and time again too.

My point is that pressure to release title deeds has been with us for a long time. If the government did not take much action over the matter when it, the property sector and the banks were being dragged through the dirt by the media, and has not taken the bulls by the horn when non-action could threaten the precarious state of the economy even more, just what on earth will it take?

June 2014

In memory of Pearl and Splodge

Once you have read this column, raise your hand if you have read it before. I can raise my hand before reading it because I have written it before. Countless times.

It's about animal poisoning and how simply not enough is being done to root out and make an example of the shops which sell poison and the people who poison animals. Poison is readily available to kill 'pests' which destroy crops. But this same poison is being spotted in picnic grounds, rural trails and is being injected into dead chickens to lure hungry animals.

Last year, the government surprised everyone by announcing that it was high time to establish a special unit that would devote itself to the protection of animals and lead the way to the prosecution of people who do not think twice about putting an animal through a cruel, painful death when they eat any of the varieties of poison on the market. Raise your hand again if you have witnessed this.

I witnessed two of my beautiful, precious cats, Pearl and Splodge, swiftly choking to death after eating poison. It was one of the most horrific things I have experienced. They had lived happily and safely in and around my home in central Paphos for ages without any trouble. I fed them and cared for them. They did not need to go and scrounge for food elsewhere. This didn't stop someone from putting poison down around my home and killing two of my pets.

Even an animal which does scrounge for food does not deserve to die in such a way.

Who put it down? I have always had my suspicions but could never prove it and this is the problem. On a happier note (if there can be one in such a situation) another of my cats was strong enough to survive the same poisoning.

Poisoning is an offence, but I think I can count on one finger the number of times anyone has come close to being charged for it. Where are the Neighbourhood Watch police that the government promised last year?

In the meantime, muzzle your dogs, carry an anti-poison kit with you at all times and take your pets for walks where none of your neighbours who hate animals will think to leave poison around.

June 2015

When choice is more than a slogan

I have been in Britain for the last few days to deal with some personal business that was signed and sealed months before the Brexit vote date was announced by the UK Prime Minister back in February. I'm happy with this coincidence as for the first time in ages I have been concerned about the political situation in the UK and was interested in being on the ground to pick up the mood of my fellow voters ahead of the June 23 vote.

By now, the outcome of the plebiscite is known, but, beforehand, the mood 'on the ground' was even less clear than in Cyprus where British ex-pats I spoke to in recent months had firm views either in support of or against Brexit. Friends and family who were sure they would vote to remain in the European Union found themselves getting cold feet about doing so. The same applied for those who were adamant that they would vote to leave.

It's not difficult to understand this state of affairs. If you knew where to look, you had half a chance of getting some fairly rounded coverage on the advantages of either staying or going (which ranged from the benefits of the peace that has prevailed in Europe since WWII and improvement in local cuisine that firm European links brought to the UK to having what has been viewed as more sovereignty) but, in a world where sound bites rule the roost, the 'campaign' was reduced to a slew of snappy-sounding phrases that insulted even the thickest person's intelligence.

Many of my circle admitted to me they had no trust for the involved politicians and were waiting for someone to come out with something sensible. Possibly somebody did, and it struggled to float in a sea of agenda-driven propaganda.

But while the FOR and AGAINST campaigns have, in my view, been rushed, cheaply emotive and disappointing, the memorabilia has been interesting. I happened to be in a part of the country where the position was for leaving the EU so practically every shop window was emblazoned with posters that bore messages supporting this, pubs had bespoke coasters challenging all EU-related institutions, restaurants produced in-house magazines that had nothing good to say about the EU and more than a few bods sported Brexit T-shirts. All these trappings dwarfed even those which supported England's participation in the European football championships.

I've picked up samples of all the above. Who knows, maybe they'll be worth something one day.

June 2016

Restful journeys

Over the last few months, I seem to have been doing more travelling than usual for both work and play. It has got to a point where I'll find myself handing over my passport at check-in in a state of mild confusion thinking to myself: "Wasn't I here just last week? Or was it yesterday?" I have become so familiar with Larnaca Airport, from where most of my recent journeys have started, that, following a few reccies, I now know where all four electricity sockets available for public use are located (useful when you need to plug in a laptop).

Taking off from Larnaca and travelling westwards during the day on a relatively routine basis has introduced me to a splendid scene that has fast become familiar: the topography of Cyprus. Cyprus is such a small island that you'd think a plane would whip over it in no time. But the view of the Troodos, plains then coast goes on for a considerable amount of time before there is nothing but an expanse of azure below and we are heading for Greece. The vista is breath-taking.

This is when I wish I was a poet, so I could do justice to the panorama of the island seen from the height of an ascending airplane. From the air, Cyprus reveals its origins as a result of the collision of the Anatolian and African Plates eons ago. It's as though a great pair of hands has scrunched up a huge sheet of paper then carefully flattened it out again leaving dramatic ranges of foothills and mountains. Lines of ridges resembling the spines of prehistoric animals spread in every direction. Ochres, greens and greys are picked out by the sunlight while geometric, sharply-defined purple shadows indicate where the rugged slopes face away from the sun. It all rises higher and higher to Mount Olympus then gives way to the vast plains which spread, beyond the mountains, northwards where the earth and air seem to blend. Eventually, it all descends to the western coast where I vainly try to pick out Paphos wineries I like, and successfully pinpoint the Akamas. Then, all of a sudden, we are over the Mediterranean Sea which, from a height appears to be of a finely ruffled texture and flecked with diamond dust.

Perhaps because I have usually travelled from Paphos or after nightfall, this unfolding east-to-west island view has not made such an impression on me before. It's a beautiful, magnificent and calming start to any journey.

June 2017

Cypriot kindness

I was walking along a back street when I came across a sight that made me slow my pace. A burly man standing on a curb side was looking down at, as I got closer and could make it out, a kitten. The kitten, about eight weeks old, was in a sorry state. It was lying in the nook of the curb and was motionless. I asked the man if it had been hit by a car. He told me that he wasn't sure. I knelt next to the kitten and saw that it didn't look injured but was very ill and weak. Perhaps it had a virus.

Carefully, we moved the kitten to a nearby patch of grass and he went to get some water which we administered with a bottle cap. This revived the kitten a bit. As we took turns stroking its head, something this rather unkempt man did very gently, he explained that he had got in touch with an acquaintance who was connected to one of the local animal charities. He had been keeping an eye on the kitten while waiting for her to arrive.

This lady got there soon afterwards, and we transferred the kitten to a cat basket while she found out what seemed to be wrong with the animal. Then she whisked it away in a car to be examined. Maybe it was too unwell to be saved. Perhaps, with the right care, it hopefully made it.

Another time, wandering around Kato Paphos I was struck by the sight of a clowder of cats (yes - that really is what a group of cats is called, along with 'glaring'). There are so many strays that you usually don't notice them, but these ones stood out as they were all pure white. A man approached with his wife and started to shake some dried food out for them while she filled disposable containers with water. We got talking and he explained how he fed felines in the neighbourhood three or four times a week although he couldn't really afford to.

He reminded me of what I would describe as the quintessential cat lady, a woman who makes it her business to do the rounds daily close to where I live, leaving a trail of food for strays. As soon as she turns in at the end of the road, the strays appear from wherever they have been lounging and weave around her ankles with their tails high.

Did I mention these people were Cypriot? I only do so because I have recently heard a wave of comments from people who have moved here from abroad about the level of animal cruelty here. I have lived here long enough to be tired of this perspective. It is true that you witness some horrible and hurtful scenarios in Cyprus. Anyone who has helplessly watched a cat or dog choke to death on poison knows what I mean. But there is also an equal amount of compassion with caring people doing what they can to make life easier for animals on the island. You only have to open your eyes.

June 2017

Café culture

Local café culture has become more appealing over the last few years. Where there used to be only a handful of spots, now there is a good choice of different places with eclectic atmospheres, making their mark.

Working remotely for all my employers, I have the choice of beavering away at my desk or spending several hours in a café and writing and editing there. Whenever I get cabin fever this is what I do. I have my favourite place and I'll head there two or three times a week. It's got to the point where the staff, all young, pleasant kids, see me come in and reel off what I want to order before I open my mouth. I've also made friends with some of the other patrons. All in all, it's what a local haunt should be.

The other day, I had been working there for a few hours and was deep in concentration. Even so, I had been aware for some time of a man sitting several tables away who was also intently working on a small pad of paper in front of him. He didn't seem to be writing but was busy doing something, so I was quite curious. At some point, perhaps half an hour later, I looked up from my laptop to see him standing in front of me proffering a piece of paper. I thought it was a leaflet promoting an event, so reached out and took it. But when I looked at it I saw that it was a pencil drawing of me sitting working. His signature was at the bottom.

For a second, I thought it was a tad creepy, but he explained, in broken English, that he had liked the scene and had wanted to draw it. Indeed, he had framed my figure with the lovely surrounding sandstone walls and vintage furniture.

The gesture touched me for reasons I can't explain, especially since he caught a look of concentration I must have when I'm working.

I couldn't decipher his signature, so I don't know what his name is, but I've seen him again at the same café and elsewhere, usually working from photographs. Keep your eye open as, one day, he might be drawing you.

I like his activity. It's like an unofficial complement to the rich programme of Pafos2017.

June 2017

Gorgeous graffiti

There are three things I refuse to lose any sleep over. One is whether Cyprus will get into the Eurovision finals next year. The second is the H1N1 virus. And the third is the graffiti on Aphrodite's Rock. Last week, we were hit with reports and photographs about the 'ugly graffiti' all over the famous lovers' rock and how the authorities should do something about it – pronto!

Now I understand the purpose of this kind of publicity. It is aimed not at solving the problem but highlighting it. And I respect the fact that the multi-coloured hearts and cupids' bows are upsetting some quarters. But these reports really surprised me because the graffiti in question is one of my favourite things about Aphrodite's birthplace.

I have a fascinating book. It's full of obscene drawings and crass flippant utterances. Before you get any misunderstanding about what I read in my spare time, I'll have you know that it's published by the American School of Classical Studies at Athens. Its title is 'Graffiti in the Athenian Agora' and it was one of the first things I pounced on when I visited the Greek capital. I love this stuff. As well as things I can't repeat here, it has translations of scribblings made by bored ancient Athenians who wrote things like 'The boy is lewd' and 'I am Thamneius'. Someone even bothered to inscribe the phrase 'Cheap Wine' onto one of the walls at the Agora. Was it a hawker's banner or just someone angry about the quality of what they'd drunk?

As I have written before in Paphos Notes, most of the worlds' population don't even know that Cyprus is The Island of Love let alone there's such a place called 'Aphrodite's Rock'. Are the same authorities that fail to exploit this tourist calling card going to push for a round-the-clock presence of an anti-graffiti guard there? How is the guard going to stride after a graffiti culprit and arrest him or her? Have you tried walking on that beach? The effort required to wade through pebbles is equivalent to four rounds of circuit training. So, I can already see we are going to need more than one guard. Of course, they will need to be paid. In short, I don't think so.

Let's make a feature of the graffiti. Isn't expressing your love for someone at such a site natural? Can we really stop it? I think it should be mentioned in the guide books: "When visiting Aphrodite's Rock make sure that you look at the multi-lingual messages inscribed from people all over the world, on the western face of the rock." And, no, the 'I love Lucy' inscription about half-way up the rock has nothing to do with me.

Date unknown

July

Job descriptions

I am never going to criticise the Electricity Authority of Cyprus (EAC) again. Not even when I get an extortionate bill for merely running my apartment.

Likewise, I am never going to grumble about my Internet provider again. Even when it cuts out five times a day, as was happening last week before the terrible explosion that claimed 13 lives at the Evangelos Florakis Naval Base on Monday.

When the blast damage caused to the neighbouring Vassilikos power station caught up, on Tuesday afternoon, with where I live in Yeroskipou, and the power cut out, I went out to do some pavement-pounding vox pops.

I had little confidence that the power would be back on two hours later and was fretting about the work load I happened to have. But, when I got home, I tested the light and the power came on. I pounced on the computer and got to work before the next cut.

I think the EAC has dealt with the electricity crisis caused by the naval inferno superbly in terms of their rotation of power and dissemination of information to the public who, after all, have to carry on with the business of living.

I can't give the same praise to the official on whose doorstep the responsibility for the blast will eventually be laid. The finger of blame hasn't settled on anyone yet but there is little doubt that they are on the government payroll. Which means that taxes are funding their undoubtedly comfortable salary.

If you earn below the tax threshold, you will be contributing to this with the VAT on your cigarettes. If you don't smoke, you will be paying with the tax on your bread and milk. This week I have truly understood with every cell in my body the meaning of the phrase 'misuse of taxpayers' money'.

Meanwhile, despite the power reductions, staff at Paphos hotels were somehow managing to attend to their duties with a smile while perspiring in shirts and ties in lobbies without air conditioning. The girl at the bakery was recording all transactions with a notebook because the till wasn't working. The staff at the Cyprus Weekly managed to get the paper out even though the facilities were severely limited as was the case with all offices across the country.

Compare this with the 'decision' (and I use the word loosely) of a tax-salaried government employee made to leave a stash of poorly-stored dangerous explosives next to a power plant.

It's reassuring to know that there are at least some individuals and companies capable of fulfilling their job descriptions.

July 2011

The case

In my hallway, there is a mid-sized, red case. Actually, I can't technically call it a case anymore because it doesn't have any handles or wheels. Its zippers are still intact though, so it could be used as a storage box. This is what I might turn it into.

There is a story behind this 'case'. I have just returned from a few days in London where I saw family and friends, listened to eccentrics at Speakers Corner, watched performance poets, attended night-long tango events, visited exhibitions and browsed in bookshops. I did so much, I can't remember it all.

I have a large case and a small case but the size I needed for my visit to London was medium. So, I went down to the luggage shops in Kato Paphos and found one on sale for €16.

"Good," I thought examining it. "It's not Samsonite but I'll get three uses out of it before it falls apart."

Three uses? I should have been so lucky. When I was on my way to Paphos airport a few days after, the top handle snapped off. "Never mind," I thought. "It still has the side handle and the back pulley."

I checked in and forgot about my case. But, at Gatwick, I had to face the fact that, in transit, the spindly pulley had been knocked out of shape and was now unusable. That left me with one side handle.

I explained all of this to my sister who met me at Victoria station from where we caught the bus up to her neighbourhood. "I hate to tell you, but I live on the fifth floor and there is no lift" she said. But at the Edwardian apartment house where she lives, my sister seized the 16.5-kilo case and ran non-stop up five flights of stairs. Again, I forgot about it. Until my second-to-last day in London.

I had decided to indulge and spend my final night at a very swish hotel on The Strand (I'll be living on lentils until the end of next year, but it was worth it). I am not a connoisseur of London hotels, so I can't say it is the best, but it is certainly one of the most renowned and I had always admired its art deco awning. With a combination of bus, taxi and prayer, I got my fragile case to the hotel. I luxuriated in the beautiful art deco room all afternoon, went out with friends, then came back to sleep on a bed made in heaven. After I checked out, my sister and I relaxed in the spacious lobby enjoying the lush, plush atmosphere and admiring the Lalique fountain. Then it was time to go to the airport.

I thought I would just make it into a taxi, but the final handle of the case broke off in front of the hotel. At Gatwick, with more prayers, I managed to check it in. As I was boarding the plane I decided to tell my sister as a joke, that the wheels had dropped off in transit.

No need to joke. When I spied it on the luggage belt at Paphos airport, I saw that the wheels really had broken off.

I don't know how I got it home, but I did because it is in my hallway. The moral of the story is never, ever under any circumstances purchase cheap luggage unless you are adept at balancing 16.5 kilos on your head.

July 2011

Razzle dazzle

Having dipped in and out of a few in my time, I personally think that casinos are some of the most boring places on earth. But I guess I am in the minority because the government projects that around 500, 000 visitors will be flocking to Cyprus once THE casino is built in…well nobody knows where yet.

I write THE casino as the state has decided, after industry consultation, that there will be one casino for all of Cyprus rather than the hoped for few dotted around with their beneficial economic side effects for the environs. However, the Paphos SEKO (the Coordinating Committee of Parties and Organisation) isn't having any of it. A meeting is planned today during which it will discuss ways of trying to convince the government to change its mind and issue licences for a casino in each district of the island.

I'm not sure that this is the right approach or that the absence of a casino in Paphos would be such a financial disaster although I understand SEKO has to put up a fight. But what precisely would the financial benefits be to the tourism sector of having a local casino? Well hotel occupancy for a start. If a casino is an added attraction for some prospective visitors, they will need to stay somewhere nearby to enjoy it. Secondly: eating and drinking. They'll need to spend money on grub. Thirdly: jobs. increased employment means a boost to the local economy.

But going back to wining and dining, would local restaurants really benefit from the presence of a casino? I don't think so. I bet (oops!) my bottom dollar that casino-goers would eat at the venue which would be akin to the all-inclusive situation that local restaurateurs say has added to their struggles. Regarding point one and three, there is a simple solution: a bus.

Casinos all over the world bus their clientele from their hotels to their doors. Cyprus is such a small island I don't see why this should be a problem for a place like Paphos. Shouldn't the town be focusing on its Culture Capital 2017 project rather than getting a casino licence? Paphos could maintain what culture it has and develop and market this alongside its easy access to the glitz of a casino. In other words, it could offer the best of both worlds; a holiday in a charming (just bear with me please) resort with a night out at the razzle-dazzle gambling venue.

One humble request to the powers-that-be from little old me though. Wherever this casino may end up being built, please please, please show some original thought and do not name it after Aphrodite.

July 2013

Make it ugly

So, yet another swimmer has drowned along the dangerous coastline in the Venus Beach area near Paphos. The latest victim was a 36-year-old man. He drowned on Monday.

What makes this drowning that bit more shocking than the relatively high number of other drownings at the same beach is the fact that the man was local. You can almost forgive the foolishness of tourists who, in spite of the warning signs peppered along this deadly beach, are probably seduced by the Mediterranean and think that it is only other people who end up drowning. But surely someone local should be aware of how dangerous this stretch of coast is. Surely someone local should know that there are plenty of safe beaches a stone's throw from this killer patch of water.

Still, I am sick to death of hearing one version or another of this story each year then having to endure the subsequent 'it's not our fault'spiel amongst different authorities which passes as a serious discussion on the matter. The latest suggestion is the construction of wave barriers to calm the currents. Of course, such a project can't be undertaken because of the economic crisis. That is the excuse now.

True, the authorities have placed huge signs warning would-be swimmers that they are entering dangerous waters at their own risk. They have positioned red-flags along the beach indicating that it is not safe and placed buoys and ropes in the waters themselves in case anyone who saunters past all of the warning signs and goes for a dip finds themselves in trouble.

But I don't know why they don't just scatter the beach with rocks and broken glass and stretches of rolled barbed wire to ram the message home that this is not a place to swim. I doubt these materials would break the bank. I don't know why the authorities don't just outright forbid it. I don't know why they don't make the beach ugly and threatening in order to reflect the reality that it is not a pleasant place. The signs etc are evidently not working. What on earth is it going to take for the powers-that-be to make sure that nobody, local or visiting, steps foot on this perilous beach again?

July 2013

Don't call me 'madam'

Yesterday, a Filipina lady stopped me on the street and asked me to help her figure out how to use an ATM. Her card wouldn't work but it turned out it was only because she was confused about the bank she was using. She was trying the right card in the wrong machine. When I pointed this out, she sort of bowed her head and said: "Thank you very much madam."

I hate this – being called 'madam'. But, like it or not, I find I am called 'madam' a lot by immigrant workers from the Philippines, Syria, Sri Lanka and Bangladesh who have come to Paphos to earn some money. They step out of my way and say, 'madam this and madam that'. They lower their eyes and say, "excuse me madam", "sorry madam". Who me? I want to say.

Most nights I take a stroll around the park at the bottom of my cul-de-sac for some cool air before going to sleep. Since the weather has started warming up, I have noticed it has become a nocturnal meeting place for several Arab families. What seems like 25, 000 kids of all sizes and ages play together gleefully on the slides and tyre swings in the comforting proximity of their mothers who sit in a ring on the ground laughing and chatting. I don't know what they are saying but, being a bunch of women, I can imagine what kind of thing it is that makes them shriek with laughter. The husbands loiter nearby talking on mobile phones or smoking. Nobody notices me. Nobody calls me madam.

It's the same in the public park in central Paphos. Yes, we all know that there is a seedy corner where ageing men park their cars, lean on the wall and stare at the foreign girls while they toss their komboloi around their fingers. I'm talking about the other part, where the Sri Lankans cook delicious spicy vegetarian food and sit with their Sunday friends. It's close to the part where the Filipino community get out the guitars and stage intimate music and dance shows for their own amusement. I walk through and, again, nobody calls me madam.

This is why I like these two parks a lot. It's restorative to see people who by day, often aren't even called their real names while slaving away subserviently for enough cash to send cheap DVD players from the budget shop back home, being what they really are: human beings.

Date unknown

August

Take a cab? I'd rather walk

Paphos taxi drivers have claimed responsibility for an arson attack on a recently-launched, petrol-powered tourist train service that runs along the Paphos seafront. A spokesman for the Paphos taxi drivers said that the union was outraged because tourists were being driven several metres along the shopping street for only €1, robbing cabbies of trade on 'their turf' and means to support themselves in their old age, send their kids to university plus blasting them out of their complacent Mercedes seats into a space where they actually have to become 'competitive'. "We've also heard rumours that the train will soon take passengers to Paphos International Airport," he said. "We're going to go to war with the government over this!"

OK - I've made this facetious little news story up. But I expect to read something similar in the papers soon. That's what this week's taxi strike was about, wasn't it? Giving the public in a free market economy what is generally called a 'choice' on the transport front? But no – the taxi drivers say that the strike was over what they call (cue violins) 'unbalanced competition' they are facing from the new airport bus services.

'Unbalanced competition'. Hmm. That sounds interesting. Can someone please define it for me? You see, maybe I'm thick, but I thought that in a free market economy there was only plain 'competition'. Well, I guess holding a 24-hour strike and blockading airport access is a step up from thumping 'rival' rickshaw drivers and, like rabid wolves, menacingly circling people who are collecting family from the airport in their own cars. Don't these blinkin' taxi drivers know that every European city has multiple means for travelling about? Here, they just have buses to compete with. What would the taxi drivers do if there were also subway trains and in the case of Venice, boat taxis too?

After I've written this I'm going to have a think about how much "unbalanced competition" I'm facing in my line of work Then I'm going to blockade the Paphos to Limassol motorway.

In case you haven't noticed, I'm not a huge fan of Paphos taxis. I would rather walk to the airport on my hands with my case balanced on my feet than hire a cab. It's not for no reason. I hate thugs. I despise people who think they're owed a living just 'because'. And I don't appreciate being charged €30 for the short journey from the airport to Yeroskipou by a taxi driver who decides that, because I'm English and a woman, I'm the ideal candidate to subsidise his shortage of earnings that night.

And it isn't that I don't sympathise with having your livelihood threatened either. I've both unexpectedly lost my income overnight and been broke once or twice and neither experience is a bowl of cherries. But, unlike many people I know personally who have walked into work this year and found that they don't have a job anymore, don't tell me for a second that the taxi drivers haven't seen the new airport bus services coming. Not just for months but for years. They have had time to adapt, branch out, prepare. And they haven't.

What did they think? That they'd just go on in their white Mercedes speeding through red lights, driving up your backside, taking over on dangerous bends and zipping over zebra crossings while someone was halfway across, unrivalled forever and ever amen? What planet are they on exactly?

Let me give you taxi drivers some tips on 'balanced competition': Stop ranting about 'unlicensed taxis' and get legal yourselves by installing meters in your cabs as you are supposed to. Quit ripping people off. Smile.

Until such a time, I would rather take the harbour choo-choo train to the airport even if I have to sit on a pile of luggage on the roof and have tree branches slapping my face all the way to the terminal.

August 2009

Front row seats

Aren't we lucky that Athens has shut down for August. Because Athens has shut down, the nightclubs aren't open and because the nightclubs aren't open, top Greek singers who normally perform there are touring the regions, including Cyprus. And when they come to Paphos, they perform at the Paphiakos Stadium, a stone's throw from where I live.

I live so close to this arena that when the floodlights are on, they illuminate a corner of my living room.

It isn't just the light that filters its way through the atmosphere into my apartment, but the sound too. So, I get to enjoy all the concerts for free from the comfort of my own balcony.

This is ideal because, I don't know if I am just getting old or this summer has been particularly oppressive, but I am doing everything in slow motion these days (and, sometimes, no motion at all).

When Anna Vissi, whom I love, performed at Paphiakos Stadium in July, I did think about getting off my backside and going to buy a ticket, but it seemed like too much effort. Lethargy won the day.

But on the night of her performance, soon after dusk, the strains of Vissi's rich, sensual voice wafted through the airwaves and landed on my balcony.

The breeze knocked the sound around a bit, but it still wasn't bad, and I savoured a free concert in my own 'box' with chilled wine on tap. The trend was set.

Last week, Despina Vandi, whom I quite like, performed. I sat on my balcony in a comfy cushioned chair with my feet up…and chilled wine on tap.

Tonight, is Sakis Rouvas' turn. To be honest, I can leave or take him. But, if nothing else comes up tonight, I'll be in the old 'box' with my wine.

So, when is somebody going to bring Leonard Cohen, Eleni Tsaligopoulou and Lara Fabian to Paphiakos Stadium? I just need to know so I can get the wine in stock.

August 2010

Cover it up

I am normally nice to tourists in these columns. But I am not going to be this week.

There is a string of beachside hotels in Kato Paphos which are connected by a pedestrian pathway winding its way through pleasant grounds. You can walk the whole length of it, stopping off for a drink or iced coffee at one of the hotel bars if you wish. I enjoy strolling along here early evening, but my stroll is often wrecked when my blood pressure goes up at the sight of a tourist strutting towards me in nothing but her bikini bottoms.

Am I the only person who finds this offensive, exhibitionist and anti-social? It is questionable enough on the beaches (none of which are nudist). But on a public walkway where you can encounter any Tom, Dick and Harry of every age, creed and nationality? Readers with XY chromosomes might not understand what I am getting so het up about, but surely it is a matter of context. Behaviour which is acceptable in one place may be utterly objectionable in another.

It has a knock-on effect too. I am convinced that the bad behaviour on Bar Street of some female tourists and the bare-breasted, brazen strutting around in inappropriate spots of others is the reason why some Cypriot men here think they are entitled to talk to foreign women who live here permanently as though they are a bunch of slappers.

Example: "Why don't we go and try out a room in that new hotel?" (invitation I received from a taxi driver.) Or: "Come around the counter and give me a kiss" (demand to one of my friends from a shop owner when she was merely collecting a fixed watch). Oh, you don't want to hear the long, long list of slimy, sleazy, suggestive, out of order, unprovoked comments that I and my friends, married and single, have been recipients of over the years.

A rule of thumb for the Cypriot men who fall into this scummy category of behaviour; if you wouldn't dare say it to a Cypriot woman, don't damn well think you can say it to anyone else.

Which leads me back to the topics of these topless perambulators. If you ladies really couldn't care less about how your half-naked parading about in the wrong places gives an unsavoury image of foreign woman, maybe you'll care about this: it's illegal. I confirmed this with the police (no doubt the query, made in my wonky and indignant Greek gave them a laugh for the day). On the beach, naked torso sun bathing is regarded as being acceptable but even if you are just half a centimetre off a beach you can be fined anywhere from €177 upwards. So, cover it up will you.

And while we're on the subject of illegal bathing non-attire, can someone please, please, please pass a ban on itsy-bitsy Speedo swimming trunks? Pretty please? Pretty, pretty please?

August 2010

Fan the flames

It was with a sick stomach that I read about the recent spate of forest fires in Paphos and Limassol Districts being the work of arsonists. These toe rags belong in the same category as animal poisoners. They are destructive cowards who are notoriously tough to track down.

It was with an even sicker stomach that I read about the fire services being about 22% down on manpower owing to early retirements. When did these happen and why weren't the retirees replaced in full or in part at least with new recruits or properly-trained reserves before the hot weather kicked in?

Every summer fires devour scrub and agricultural land. Whether they are started deliberately or not is neither here nor there. What are the authorities thinking to allow the fire-fighting force go through the hottest months of the year without a full quota of manpower? That's not to say that the fire brigade and supporting services don't do splendidly when dealing with the blazes that are a feature of summer in Cyprus. Nobody can ignore the water-carrying helicopters which fly low over Paphos giving a tell-tale sign that there are teams of fire-fighters dealing with an inferno somewhere. I think everybody down here on the ground is always rooting for them.

In day-to-day reality, surely the fire-fighting services are more important than the National Guard. They should be funded and manned as such.

Also, the services are recruiting the assistance of volunteers who will help in preventing fires through passing on information about blazes as early as possible. This sounds good but how to assess which fires need immediate attention and which can wait if the information is coming from well-meaning but inexperienced volunteers?

The fire-fighting services should have all the funds and staff necessary at their disposal to fulfil their duties thoroughly and safely. No questions asked.

August 2013

Change needed

Something very upsetting was shoved into my face last week.

I had the pleasure of doing a write up about what Paphos has to offer on the beach and archaeology front. As you can imagine, it was pretty enjoyable reminding myself about the range of beaches in the area and all of the antiquity riches which are free or incur a low entrance fee for access. The upsetting thing about it all though, which was repeated time and time again, was the limited or no access to these delights for wheelchair users.

I've picked up bits and pieces over the years about how this site has had an upgrade to make it more accessible for people with limited mobility and that beach has a special ramp for people in wheelchairs. For this reason, I was under the false impression that there had been some improvement and a move in the right direction for making the tourist side of Paphos friendly for disabled visitors.

How wrong I was. There is limited access for wheelchair users to a mere two sites in Paphos District; the Roman Mosaics and the Tombs of the Kings. In a way, I can understand the limitations imposed for anyone trying to create a wheelchair friendly infrastructure on archaeological sites. After all, if my experience is anything to go by, even if you're fully mobile, walking around ancient sites can be taxing because they're old. The surfaces are uneven, you have to clamber up and down millennia-old steps and squeeze through narrow openings. But only two sites? Out of the scores in the area?

It was the same story for the beaches. I was sure at some point Yeroskipou Beach used to have a sea-entry ramp for wheelchair users to enjoy the Mediterranean. I didn't see it the last time I was there and could find no record of it on the Cyprus Tourism Organisation (CTO) website.

At least the CTO does have a downloadable booklet advising disabled visitors and their companions about what to expect in Cyprus. It details which tourist spots are accessible for wheelchair users and gives advice about available transport and places to stay for visitors with limited mobility. But it's only 12 pages long. And in those 12 pages the print is large and there are loads of photographs. The information for Paphos is scanty. According to the booklet, not one local beach is fitted out for wheelchair users. Not one of the local museums is either. The two aforementioned archaeological sites are, which isn't bad because there are only five in total across the island which do have disabled access.

I thought Paphos had come on a bit in this department. Not so. It's not just for visitors either. What about people who live here?

August 2014

Extremes

The announcement by Hermes airports this week that it would open its check-in areas to the public, travellers or not, to serve as cooling centres when temperatures went past 40 reminded me of another extreme situation at the other end of the scale.

I was visiting family in Toronto a couple of Christmases ago when an ice storm took the power out across half of the city for up to ten days. When it is minus 20 outdoors, the cold soon infiltrates through the walls of your home and before you know it, you have donned all of your warmest clothing, your breath hangs in the air and you have to heat up water on a camping stove.

As with the extreme heat we have been experiencing in Cyprus, this type of cold can be very serious. The Red Cross immediately set up 'warming centres' to take care of people as each day passed and power was not restored. We spent Christmas Eve in one of these places. There were facilities to sleep and bathe, hot meals and drinks and even board games and films were laid on to keep everyone entertained. You could stay for as long as you needed absolutely free of charge – and many did until the electricity was back on and it was warm enough to go back home.

Sitting in Paphos these last few days, feeling like I am in a hammam, I now cannot begin to imagine what that type of cold felt like and would have happily spent a minute or two in minus zero temperatures. I am not a lover of air-conditioning so make do with a fan and open window. I can just about grin and bear it this way.

Going back to Hermes, I think they deserve a pat on the back for their initiative. They told me that the reason for opening the airports to the general public (and offering cold drinks and free parking) was because many people could not afford air conditioning and would find the afternoon hours unbearable as the heat wave continued. I know that, in the capital, a few community centres have also invited vulnerable people like the elderly to simply go around and sit in a cool spot.

What I'd like to know is why the local authorities haven't laid such facilities on? We all knew that there was going to be a heat wave.

August 2015

Saving the turtles

Last weekend I finally got around to doing something that I have meant to do for years. I joined the Young Greens in a beach clean-up at Lara where two types of endangered turtles, the Green and Loggerhead, nest.

This activity has been going on for about 15 years and is open to non-party members. This year I was determined to join in so signed up and prepared for a couple of hours of picking up rubbish. There was also a chance we would see some baby turtles.

Green and Loggerhead turtles have been declared, by the World Conservation Union as endangered and both are protected under a number of conventions. They have been protected in Cyprus since 1971 but development and rubbish-strewn beaches have interfered with their breeding. Turtles come back to where they were born to nest. If they find their home has turned into a holiday village, they probably end up dumping their eggs in the sea. Rubbish is hazardous as they can chew on it and choke.

If they do manage to nest, the baby turtles hatch about 60 days later and emerge at night. They head to the lightest spot which is the horizon of the sea. They then begin their life in the oceans and can, if they survive the perils or predators and fishing nets there, live much longer than a human being.

Dealing with rubbish is where we came in over the weekend. A sizeable crew collected a huge heap of rubbish bags full of plastic, metals and clothing discarded by bathers and campers. The Young Greens make a record of everything that is picked up in order to monitor cleanliness. We had to check off items on a pre-printed list. Reading some of the items we could be expected to come across, I wondered what I had let myself in for. In the end I was, perhaps, fortunate though. Most of my trash bags were filled with plastics of some sort.

After our work, we were rewarded with the sight of several baby turtles. Nests are marked by small wire enclosures and one had evidently been vacated. An expert on our team dug a little deeper and found a few eggs remaining and, among these, there were four or five baby turtles ready to emerge. We helped them on their way by placing them close to the shore and, although they struggled a bit with the waves, they eventually disappeared into the Mediterranean.

If one of them survives, it will be swimming in the oceans decades from now after we're all gone. Who knows who will be running for the US presidency then, what state the EU will be in or who the celebrities of the day will be.

August 2015

Strange beaches

A few weeks ago, I wrote about the charms of Paphos beaches but the most memorable beach I have ever been to is on the edges of Varosha on the opposite side of the island in Famagusta.

It has the crystal-clear water beaches for which Cyprus has been awarded so many Blue Flags, and its enviably rich golden sand, for which beaches from this enclave all the way up to the tip of the Karpas are famous, leaves many a Paphos beach wanting.

The beach at Famagusta is memorable not only for its natural characteristics, but the man-made ghost town surrounding it. A spot allocated for swimmers is overlooked by deteriorating hotels, lift shafts exposed, signage faded, abandoned during the 1974 Turkish invasion. These are cordoned off by a ramshackle fence that disappears into the sea at the beach edge and is met by a broken string of buoys. This creates a gaping gap through which anyone can swim into the restricted zone. Nobody is supposed to swim beyond this point into Varosha proper. If you do, a policeman, seated in a make-shift tower, blows a whistle at you. But, despite the broken sea barrier, an invisible barricade is very strong as, when I visited, nobody ventured beyond this watery line.

In fact, it was as though they were not on a beach being stared at by the empty eyes of vacated hotel rooms and buildings preserved in an ugly, traumatic moment of the island's recent history. A group of boys held a diving contest at a mysteriously deep spot at the beachside, families picnicked and listened to music, children snorkelled, and tourists sunbathed.

What has always struck me over the years as efforts towards a Cyprus solution have been undertaken, is there has been little consideration about how one of the island's chief economic activities, tourism, would be impacted. Specifically, how would Paphos, already competing with Larnaca, compete with the likes of beautiful sandy Famagusta and the Karpas? Likely such matters are secondary concerns to the return of Morphou and a political makeup. Anyway, competition is always a good thing. But it's worth noting that when Famagusta was a developed, sophisticated tourism destination before the events of 1974, Paphos had one, maybe two hotels.

Many Cypriots, mostly Nicosians, have said to me that Paphos was least hurt by the invasion because, with the precarious situation in the occupied areas, suddenly local tourism flourished. While Varosha fell into ruin, Paphos visitor numbers grew.

Any success Paphos has had has not been handed to the district. The local tourism authority is very active in promoting the area and attracting airlines and anyone knows what hard work the hospitality sector needs.

But, if there is a solution or even simply a resolution to the Cyprus problem, how will Paphos tourism fare in the longer term?

August 2017

Learning from Paphos

How interesting to hear Nicosians themselves finally assess the capital as somewhat lacking when it comes to being a tourist pull. Last week the Nicosia Board of Tourism described the capital as needing a 'spruce up' both physically and culturally plus better coordination amongst municipalities for furtherment of the city's image as a spot for which it is worth making a detour from the beaches.

While my work is in Paphos, I spend time regularly in Nicosia. I fully concur with the appraisal of the capital's stakeholders. I enjoy Paphos and Nicosia for different reasons. Paphos has its natural beauty and relaxed lifestyle. But, when Paphos' insularity becomes too much, I feel grateful for my links to Nicosia. Apart from my personal connections there, I enjoy its cosmopolitan feel, chic wine bars, tango scene, wonderful old, family confectioners and the old city and its history.

But, for a capital city, it lacks a vibrant, beating heart, both physically and culturally.

I was telling one of my born-and-bred Nicosian friends about life in Paphos – especially the positive impact of the Pafos2017 European Culture Capital title. His immediate remark was that Paphos, out of all the urban centres in Cyprus, sounded like it had the most to offer residents. I am not Cypriot and have none of the partisan sentiments I see in Paphians about their home. The rivalry amongst Cyprus cities does not interest me. So, it is my completely impartial view that Paphos, indeed, has, out of all the Cypriot towns, the most to offer its residents. I think this is largely because of Pafos2017.

While some of the town's infrastructure has not been ready for the prestigious title, the programming itself has been faultless. There has been a vibrant mix of world-class acts and grassroots innovation that has incorporated not only the most populated areas of the district but villages. More importantly, the title has enabled focus on a district-wide vision. It was clear to me some way along the years-long bid for the title that Paphos was in the running to win. I don't think the other cities made as much effort as Paphos. I think there was one reason for this: complacency.

Perhaps Nicosia, as the capital of Cyprus, could look to its 'humble' neighbour for ideas on how to 'spruce up' its image and not only make it more attractive to visitors but to residents too.

August 2017

Watermelon woes

In the same way the lengthening days and first summer visit to the beach are uplifting, I always find the appearance of seasonal watermelons a welcome sight. They simply broadcast summer. Their green striped coats look so fresh, especially since you know they're hiding the promise of red, juicy, thirst-quenching, flesh within.

The mountains of watermelons you encounter at every supermarket, froutaria and even being hawked at the roadside during this season, give you a sense of summertime abundance. You start imagining endless litres of refreshing, chilled watermelon juice and bottomless supplies of cooling, sweet slices of this generous fruit heaped up on a plate that practically replenishes itself until the hot weather fades (and somehow this eventuality is impossible to imagine).

With the positive vibes that the first watermelons emanate, I find it difficult to imagine there will come a day, round about the start of August, when I'll be sick to high heaven of them. But that day is here. I've simply got tired of trying to come up with imaginative things to do with them (because somehow even though they're delicious, watermelon juice and chunks get plain repetitive).

Why do I buy watermelon then you might ask? At this stage in the summer, most of the time I don't. I get given it by friends and neighbours who are, apparently, experiencing a surplus. Why not say no to their offers? The answer is so obvious I barely see the sense in writing it: you just don't say no to such things in Cyprus. You accept the watermelon with a smile and a thanks and wonder where you're going to stuff it in your fridge.

Anyway, it seems I'm not the only one who has this shaky relationship with this bountiful summer fruit. Overwhelmed by a few mammoth wedges in my fridge not to mention a bag of frozen chunks stashed in my freezer, I started searching for inventive ideas about what to do with an excess of watermelon. Seems there is an organisation in the States that is dedicated to all things watermelon related. It's called the National Watermelon Promotion Board and it has a website full of recipes for all kinds of bevvies and bites; cocktails, breakfast, appetisers, salads and side dishes.

You just can't believe what these folks have come up with. There are some fairly obvious suggestions like watermelon gazpacho and nachos with watermelon guacamole. Not so obvious are BBQ grilled spicy watermelon slices, watermelon rind stir fry and - one for the Brits - fish and chips with watermelon reduction. It's amazing how creative you can be with the humble watermelon.

Happy watermelon days! Enjoy them while they last.

August 2017

September

If you can't stand the heat

Although I am not very good at it, I like cooking. I go through flurried, frenzied phrases of trying out new French, Italian, Cypriot and Indian recipes and forcing the results onto whomever is handy.

As it happens, since April, I have been working from home for all the outfits I write for. One of the advantages of this is I can do something civilised each day which is food related. This civilised thing is called 'making lunch'. And actually eating at a table with crockery, cutlery, a glass of water and a serviette. This as opposed to stopping at a bakery on the way to the office and buying an overpriced, greasy, unhealthy pastry that normally gets consumed in front of a computer with its paper bag serving as a dish – which is, more or less hitherto, what I had been doing.

My domestic goddess routine went (note the use of the past tense) something like this: I'd beaver away all morning on my writing then, at two in the afternoon, clock off and get cooking. The nutmeg, turmeric, coconut milk, cloves, tagliatelle, garlic, cream and garam flour would all come out in one combination or another and I'd concoct a relatively exotic dish. Once I impressed myself no end by making puff pastry from scratch. The 'hausfrau' in me was always satisfied by these efforts because a) I saved money, b) what I made had something of nutritional value and c) it was civilised (something which is very important to me in the rush of modern life).

Fast forward to August and this culinary phase was swiftly and brutally assigned to the past tense. Do not ask me what I have been living on over the last four weeks of heat and humidity. I really don't know. I make filter coffee in the morning then it is all downhill from there. I have a hazy confused memory of downing glass after glass of water along with bags of crisps. I tell myself this for the salt, but it has more to do with the fact that I can't be bothered to shop, let alone cook. My herbs and spices haven't seen the light of day for weeks and the thought of washing a bunch of grapes or slicing a tomato just seems too overwhelming.

The heat keeps hunger at bay until the sun goes down at around 8pm when I am suddenly ravenous and all I can be bothered to do is make popcorn. On top of all this, I have found myself reverting to stopping at a bakery and buying a greasy, unhealthy pastry that normally gets consumed in front of a computer. The only difference between this and the former routine is that I serve it on a plate rather than a paper bag.

A message for all of you who have been lucky enough to have been fed properly during this brutal, draining, sopping wet heat: never, ever take for granted the people who shop and slave away at the stove for you. Ever! I'm sick of this astronaut's diet of H2O and vacuum-sealed salted carbohydrates. Roll on autumn, cold floors and drafts under the door. I want to get back to my French(ish) cooking.

September 2011

15 years in Aphrodite's fishbowl

Scavengers

Why is the state so darn tardy dealing with matters that concern death? It's nearly the end of 2014 and we're still waiting for a perpetually put off decision about a Bill on cremation on the island.

Now the state is dragging its feet over the number of allegedly unlicensed funeral homes in Cyprus. Bona fide funeral home directors have been canvassing the government for a little while now for stricter regulation on the running of funeral homes. They claim that out of 30 funeral homes on the island only five are run to a professional standard. They claim that many facilities are staffed with untrained people who do not know how to deal with a dead body and may, therefore, run the risk of spreading infections from the deceased. I think this could be a tad alarmist as nothing major has happened to date but there's a first time for everything, so they could have a point.

They also point to millions of euros in revenue being lost to the state because of unlicensed affairs. I am beginning to wonder if the government could care less about making the effort to accrue funds for its much-depleted coffers (think of the money lost through non-issue of thousands of title deeds which, by the way, under Troika stipulations is meant to be concluded within the next three months). It seems to be easier to clamp down on taxes, increase VAT, establish a company tax and raise the level of Social Security contributions with self-employed people suffering the most (oh, how well treated and incentivised are the wealth generating entrepreneurs of society).

But forget about cash. I would have put the issue of ethics top of the list when it comes to funeral homes which are badly run. From what I hear (and my jaw goes through the floor at what I hear about these places) the name 'Scavengers' would be more apt for these shoddily run, money-motivated variety of funeral homes. Bodies carted around like they are sacks of potatoes; staff descending on hospitals immediately after a death and harassing the distraught relatives for the body; the spouting of all kinds of unfounded laws and regulations in order to secure the corpse without giving the family time to consider any other option; jewellery – er – going missing. It's the kind of thing you'd expect to read in a Victorian novel about the underworld. This has all been communicated to me from people (the bona fide ones) in the business.

When you think that many of these people who end up in the hands of tackily-managed funeral homes wouldn't have even wanted to be buried in the first place, i.e. those from countries where cremation is the norm, it gets even more disgusting. Which leads me to the business of cremation; what on earth is going on with this Bill?

September 2014

Squeak, squeak

I do not understand people who dislike the local sweet, donut-like loukoumades. They are light, crispy yet fluffy, and not sickly. So, you would perhaps think 'lucky me' that I was a member of a party seated close to the loukoumades maker at the 9th Cyprus-Russia Gala at the Presidential Place last weekend.

One of the reasons for the event is to celebrate the business and cultural ties between the two countries and, as always, there was a splendid array of entertainment put on by gifted Cypriot and Russian performers. The evening commenced with a goose bump-making rendition of The Dying Swan by none other than prima ballerina, Svetlana Zakharova of the Bolshoi.

As the music ebbed and flowed and the dancer performed this famous scene, an unusual sound emerged and carried across the entranced audience to the stage. "Squeak, squeak," it went. A quick glance around revealed that the source was the loukoumades maker. Apparently, he had run out of dough and had to quickly churn out a few dozen balls into his boiling oil. Unfortunately, his machine was rusty.

The same thing happened during the First Lady's welcoming address. Many a disapproving glance was cast his way.

But, as the evening wore on, it became hard to dislike the loukoumades maker and his squeaking dough machine. Maybe it was the wine or the general bonhomie, but he started to become a mini-mega star himself with people filming and photographing him on their phones.

He was good humoured about it, but he kept very focused on what he was doing. He churned out gazillions of loukoumades to the hundreds of guests, heaping them up in bowls for them to be whisked away by waiters. The need for replenishment was non-stop. For four hours there was a fresh batch bubbling and browning away in his pan.

So, thank you Mr Loukoumades for adding a uniquely Cypriot character to the evening. Your fare was delicious, and I wouldn't even ask you to oil your machine next time.

September 2015

Goodbye Jasmitha

The last time I saw Jasmitha Maharajasingh, it was the late summer of 2008. She was walking through the sliding doors in the arrivals section of Larnaca Airport, dressed in pink. She was a sort of miracle which had united so many communities in Paphos as they strove to raise hundreds of thousands of euros for her brain surgery for removal of a malignant tumour.

When I saw her, she had just arrived back from Israel following ten months of treatment. You wouldn't have thought it by looking at her though. She just seemed like any other excited little girl arriving back home. Perhaps the only sign that something special was happening was the small welcome party who were greeting her.

It was heart-breaking to learn that Jasmitha died this week. Details about her condition are sketchy, but the 15-year-old was taken to Paphos hospital with breathing difficulties and transferred to Nicosia General Hospital last week. In spite of good care there, she passed away on Monday.

I remember how phenomenal it was how quickly people in Paphos and beyond rallied around the drive to raise the huge sum of money needed to get treatment for the then, six-year-old Jasmitha. Her mother was a housemaid and it was out of the question that she would be able to raise the money herself. It would have been out of the question for most people. Almost overnight it seemed that everyone was putting on an event or raffle or dinner in support of the little girl. In a short space of time, enough money was raised for the treatment to proceed.

It felt like everyone was waiting with bated breath the day the surgery was scheduled, and it seemed like everyone breathed a collective sigh of relief when it was successful. Reports came back from Israel over the following ten months about how Jasmitha was doing and to hear she was getting better and stronger was always uplifting.

Over the years I have occasionally thought about Jasmitha and wondered how and where she was. Of course, it wouldn't have been difficult to find out, but I didn't want to somehow. She had survived brain surgery and come through a gruelling course of treatment. Let sleeping dogs lie, I thought.

My heart sincerely goes out to Jasmitha's parents. I am sure I am not alone.

September 2015

Aggressive women drivers

Over the next seven days, Cyprus is taking part in European Mobility Week, putting car-free, communal, pedestrian and bicycle transport at the forefront of civil life.

The aim, of course, is to show how beneficial it can be to leave your car at home from time to time and enjoy pedestrianised areas in the town centre plus the pleasures and freedoms of cycling. But enjoying walking and cycling – two prongs of European Mobility Week – both partly depend on considerate and careful motorists, a group which is not evident in such high quantities.

As a daily urban walker, I can vouch for this. Behind the wheel, young men have a bad reputation for being reckless (and, statistically, this is fair enough). Pensioners have recently come under scrutiny for needing more stringent checks to identify physical limitations that can affect driving (most pensioners I know are better drivers than I am, but I suppose the odd one slips through the net).

But there's a third group that somehow never seems to get shown in an unsavoury light, even though, in my experience, they are some of the most anti-social town drivers: women.

Before anyone who is not in the habit of reading between the lines takes umbrage, I am not referring to every single woman on the roads in Cyprus. However, if a car nearly takes off the first layer of my skin when it tears around a corner or shoots over a zebra crossing when it shouldn't, its driver is usually someone with XX chromosomes.

The image I associate with these encounters is that of a stony, rigid profile as the car passes and the driver pretends they didn't just nearly crush my foot or, at the very least, shock the daylights out of me.

Just a few days ago, I was crossing at lights that were red for vehicles and green for pedestrians, and yet a woman tore right over the junction as I was halfway across.

Did this stupid person not realise that if she hit someone at the speed she was going at, she would maim or even kill them?

It's as if these ladies – in what comes across as a form of passive aggression – feel they're entitled to do whatever the hell they want. But there's no place for entitlement, nor, in the case of the aforementioned young men, uncontrolled testosterone on the road.

September 2016

Keep a lid on it

Winter has its cosy charms, spring is uplifting, and summer gives license for indulgence but my favourite season in any country I have lived in is autumn. Cyprus is no exception. The days gradually become shorter but, in Paphos, the autumn sunsets over the sea are atmospheric every day of the season.

I pity my friends who tell me they feel depressed when they start to see dying vegetation and register the change in the light that are signs that summer is over, and autumn's arrival is only a few weeks away. These same changes that make them feel flat make me happy. The very slight drop in the temperature is also a relief, not least of which because the reek of garbage piled up in rubbish vats on the street goes from nauseating to merely noticeable.

It never fails to amaze me how some people deal with their trash in Paphos. Cyprus is a hot country so where is the consideration to people living nearby in tossing rubbish, bagged or, even worse, unbagged, into the public vats that are dotted around the streets – without pulling the lid to a close afterwards? In the warmth, it doesn't take long for this refuse to start reeking to high heaven. Often, it's so bad, your instinct is to cover your mouth with a hanky when you pass.

Garbage gets generated regardless of scheduled rubbish pick-ups so, of course, gets tossed into these bins day and night and festers for days before collection. Not only do people throw their putrid garbage into these bins without sealing them afterwards, they sometimes pile trash in a heap so that, even if someone wanted to, they couldn't shut it. Sometimes it's the fault of the bin. It's wonky in some way and simply won't close no matter how much you yank at it which makes you think it's time for a better, more hygienic design. Some don't even have lids.

These public bins are usually positioned for communal use in spots where there are apartment buildings. There is always an unlucky tenant whose flat is a stone's throw from these open rubbish piles and the smell must be revolting. Solutions could be increased rubbish collections and more and better bins, but a start could be employing the lid for its design function and, where possible, actually shutting it.

September 2017

Gossipsville

I know that Mr. X from Tala has just asked his wife for a divorce because he objects to how her Swarovski collection is taking over the house. I also know that Mr. Y has come out, but he and his wife have decided to stay married for the children and Joe Bloggs from Peyia is a closet alcoholic and Josephine Bloggs takes Valium to get through the day. I know that Mr. So-and-So's bits don't….er…function properly because an acquaintance who got friendly with him kindly informed me.

I don't want to know any of these things. I mean, if I have never laid eyes on Joe Bloggs and Mr. So-and-So, how can I be privy to such intimate information about their private lives? This is a rhetorical question because I do know how I know these scurrilous bits of information. Gossipy ex-pats, of which there seems to be a proliferation in Paphos, think nothing of sitting in public and disrespectfully discussing, in braying voices, other people's private lives as though they are merely talking about the exchange rate.

Then there are the tongue waggers who plonk themselves down and proceed to gibber on without any discretion about … oh, you can only just imagine. "Never, ever tell another person anything in this town," I warn myself, incredulous as they rattle on at me about aforementioned Mr. So-and-So's problems.

Then, it occurred to me, if I know Mr. X is divorcing over a Swarovski collection and Josephine Bloggs takes Valium…what do people know, or think they know about me? Nothing, I would think. For one thing, I can't imagine there is anything about me or my rather mundane life that would resemble gossip fodder. For another, I keep a low profile in Paphos. But maybe that's naïve of me.

From time to time, I have a clear out and take things to the second-hand shop of one of the big charities. Amongst the books and knickknacks, I once took a large jar of coins a friend had given me in one of their clear outs. I figured someone who knew about these things might find something interesting or worth keeping.

A couple of months later, I returned to the shop with more stuff. "You were in asking about that jar of coins you brought before, weren't you?" the shop assistant told me. "Pardon?" I replied. Apparently, according to 'someone' behind the scenes at the shop, some of the coins had turned out to be valuable and I had gone back to stingily reclaim them, changing my mind about donating them.

It was untrue. I had forgotten about them. Either the 'someone' was mistaken, hallucinating or just telling porkies. And possibly pocketing the valuable coins themselves under the guise that I'd gone and retrieved them I thought, starting my own private chain of gossip.

If someone is telling fibs about me over a jar of blinkin' coins that I gave to a charity shop, what else might people concoct? So, I'd like to take this opportunity to tell you that anything unsavoury you may have heard about me is untrue. Except the story about me murdering my eighth husband and chucking his body into the Thames estuary. That's why I fled to Cyprus. Don't tell Interpol.

Date unknown

October

Warning: Santa is in town

I had a nightmare. In this nightmare, I drove to a supermarket and parked. When I emerged from my car, I discovered that I was at the foot of a Christmas tree that was a good deal taller than a parking lot lamp post. I looked towards the entrance of the supermarket and spotted a chunky, mammoth Santa sitting on the roof. He was staring straight at me with huge, circular, coal black eyes. As I cautiously entered the supermarket, I became aware that crimson Christmas decorations the size of sputniks were suspended from every inch of the ceiling. That's when I started hyper-ventilating. "Christmas," I thought to myself and took a deep breath to calm down. "Christmas is coming soon and, as usual, I have no idea what I'm doing."

As I pushed the trolley around the aisles I considered my December 25th options. Should I lie in bed all day eating chocolates and reading trashy novels? Or should I be civilised and dress up for Christmas dinner with friends? Maybe I should visit my family and have a traditional holiday for once. No – better avoid sentimentality and stay in Cyprus and just…ignore it. Or what about...?

I wish I could say that I woke up from this nightmare, but I can't. Because it was, in fact, reality. This is what I experienced at one of the Paphos supermarkets – and they're all guilty – when I did my shopping on October 31st! I hadn't even put my jack 'o lantern out let alone turned it into pumpkin soup, and the supermarkets were telling me to start panicking about Christmas?

Do you know how long away Christmas is? December 25th is eight Cyprus Weeklies away. December 25th is long enough away for a cat to get pregnant and have her kittens. Stephanie Solomonides, the Cypriot who has just left Cyprus to make the long trek across the vastness of Antarctica, will nearly be at the South Pole by the time Christmas comes. And I have to put up with Santa staring me down when I go shopping on Halloween?

Correct me if I'm wrong but, in Cyprus isn't November 14th the traditional time for donning shops with Christmas garb? Well, it looks like Santa has turned into such an egotist that he has to hog the limelight from witches and pumpkins.

October 2009

Mystery woman

One of my friends recently lost his wife to this merciless disease cancer.

His loss and what he and his wife went through are now hitting him hard. He experiences some very bad days. On top of the emotional roller coaster he is on, he has at least three women on his trail making 'romantic' gestures towards him.

One of them is a former home help, the other his current cleaning lady and the third a friend of hers. "I can't stand it," he tells me. "They all keep asking me when I'm going to ask them out. I know they just want my passport. I don't want to know, but I bet some blokes in my position would be vulnerable."

The worst thing is two of them attended his wife's funeral and the third was hitting on him within a week of the event.

When he has told me about fending off unwanted advances, misery is etched all over his face. Until, one day, he came to me with his face lit up and a plan.

"I've put a lady's magazine on the night table in the spare room and a bit of my wife's make-up in the en-suite. I'll tell you what happens."

It worked like a dream. The cleaning lady disseminated the information to her friends and they all started interrogating him about his new lady friend.

"She's just a friend who stays over sometimes" he told them ambiguously.

I soon got roped into it. I produced a tub of facial cream and a bottle of nail varnish with careful instructions about where to place them. The report that came back a few days later was encouraging. One of his 'suitors' informed him that she no longer wanted to go out with him.

This spurred me on. I raided my closet and pulled out a pair of red and black stilettos and, from the bathroom, a scarlet red lipstick. "These will get them talking," I said. He listened carefully as I told him where to put them. He then explained how he had removed the lady's magazine to give the impression if it being thrown out after being read and put bits of mascara on cotton balls then chucked them in the garbage can. I was impressed.

The next report that came back was even more encouraging than the first. One of his 'suitors' was asking him if his lady friend was 'so-and-so' or perhaps 'so-and-so'.

The other asked if he paid her! Both were less ardent in their pursuit.

I have just dug out more clothing for him to scatter around the guest room.

Any gentleman out there who want any feminine advice on how to get shed of some woman who is after your passport, I am happily at your service.

Just so long as I get my stilettos back.

October 2011

Taking the bus

I have been doing an experiment in car-free living. I have always loved the liberty and pleasure of getting from A to B on foot. I also enjoy the freedom of not worrying about where to park or if a fellow driver is going to bash into my vehicle when I leave it somewhere. Also, a relief to relinquish are the frustrating traffic jams where just about every vehicle in a congested lane contains one person and the control of road rage when someone cuts you off or doesn't offer the courtesy of indicating.

I can reach most spots I need on a regular basis by foot, the very occasional lift from a friend and an even more occasional taxi. The rest I can manage by public transport.

I grew up and spent my early adulthood in places where there is no stigma attached to taking public transport, unlike in Cyprus where my impression is using it is akin to an admission of failure and poverty. I have always seen hopping on a bus or subway train as a relatively economical convenience which is preferable to navigating a car around increasingly congested streets.

However, my experiment does not look like it's set to last much longer, and I'll explain why; I don't enjoy the experience of being a passenger on the local buses. Although there are a couple of sweeties, many of the drivers are peasants and some of the buses are from the ark.

I had to complain about one driver with anger management issues who was shrieking at me (while meant to be concentrating on driving) over my sin of being confused about where to get my ticket from. I thought he was going to have a cardiac arrest. I saw another losing his cool with an elderly lady who had to ask more than once if she was getting off at the right stop. Another time I was stunned to hear a driver shouting at a group of happy friends taking a bus to the beach on their day of freedom – Sunday – because he claimed they were chatting too loudly. They weren't but that didn't stop him from telling them to shut up – twice. "Blah, blah, blah" he rudely barked at them. Of course, when the bus driver feels like talking loudly on his mobile for the duration of the trip (something that is banned) we all have to put up with it.

I am also beginning to find the buses themselves intolerable. It is a matter of luck whether you get a clean seat with a seatbelt or an ancient one with half a seatbelt and a view of the defunct ashtrays on the back of seats plastered with eons of discarded chewing gum. In short, you alight from the bus feeling like a pleb.

So, germinating in my mind is the thought of going back to car ownership and joining the throngs of one passenger-driver vehicles clogging up the roads.

October 2015

Refugees and the unbridgeable cultural gap

I lived in Peyia a few years ago and I had some Syrian neighbours: a husband and wife and some younger brothers who were saving money to build a house back home. They were hospitable, polite and helpful. I have found this of all the Syrians I have met both in Paphos and in Syria. I have always loved the Middle East and, considering the entire region is so culturally rich, I mysteriously like Syria the most. Today, I simply cannot bring myself to read about what is happening to Palmyra.

But one day, the older brother came and sat in my living room and, in a nut-shell, dogmatically instructed me to 'stop seducing his younger brother'. I was gobsmacked. The younger brother was friends with everyone in the neighbourhood and when he visited me it was to rant about his teenage woes. I did not dignify the assumptions with a response and pretended not to know what he meant. It offended me deeply and ended our friendship.

I describe this kind of scenario as unbridgeable culture clash. This is why I have no problem with Interior Minister's statement on preferring Christian refugees to come from Syrian refugee camps to Cyprus. We like to be around people like ourselves. Wrongly or rightly.

I think the lack of information about who may be joining European countries from refugee camps and how exactly they will be integrating (and I hear a lot about this from my sister in the UK, one of several EU countries which has experienced terrorist attacks and threats in the last 10 years) is making people nervous. But if you express any reticence about the management of the refugees, you risk being called a racist, a xenophobe or some other type of limited degenerate.

Refugees need all the help they can get, and the children should be first. Anyone who can help, should.

But this refugee crisis is not a one-way conversation. The taxpayers and citizens of hosting countries have opinions and fears as well and these need to be heard. Calling someone every name in the book because they do not blindly enthuse about welcoming refugees is not going to get anyone – the unfortunate migrants or hosting peoples – anywhere.

October 2015

It really is all Greek to me

In the same way that painting the Forth Bridge in Scotland is a job that is never completed, and they start planning the next Notting Hill Festival in London the minute the last one is over, I am eternally trying to improve my Greek.

Someone should name a perennial plant or flower after the never-ending process. Or maybe a mild chronic medical condition would be better suited.

I write this now because 'tis the season to go back to school. After summer, all the lessons start again, all the books come out, all the CD sets are purchased, and the fascinating, rich local lingo is delved into by well-meaning, keen students who want to forge a deeper connection to Cyprus than they would otherwise.

I have my good days and my bad days with Greek. I enjoy the language but understand it far better than I can speak it. I have finally, though, got to a point where I have convinced myself that Greek is not so difficult and that I can improve with some commitment. This is a darn sight better than having the hitherto feeling of being defeated before I began. Of eternally being at base camp on Mount Everest with the peak so far away and an inhospitable landscape of genitive, vocative singular, accusative plural, masculine, feminine and neuter grammatical characteristics to clamber over and master en route. Lord – pass me the oxygen.

However, there's one thing that would encourage me greatly on my epic quest to improve my Greek; Cypriots, please stop speaking English to me.

I will chat to anyone in Greek for an excuse to practice. When a girl outside a perfume shop hands me a scented strip of paper in the UK, I will take it and walk on. Here I will stop, sniff it and ask questions about the fragrance. When I go into a bank in the UK, I will speak in a sort of Morse code to say what I want. Here I will use every possible relevant word I know and use full sentences. Here, I scramble around for small talk topics at cafés so I can exchange a few words with the waiter. In the UK, I am a woman of few words when ordering coffee.

I can't tell you how frustrating and undermining it is when in situations like the above, the replies immediately come back in English. When I am trying to speak Greek and the responses are in English what it says to me is: "your Greek is so poor I can't bear to listen to you ordering a filter coffee, so let's make life easy for both of us and I'll speak your mother tongue why don't I?"

How am I ever supposed to have the confidence to eventually talk about quantum physics in Greek if nobody will even let me ask to make a cash deposit at the bank?

Still, come to think of it, they did actually finish painting the Forth Bridge so there is hope.

October 2016

New anti-smoking laws

I thank god that I am not a smoker in the same way I thank god that I am not a brand-name lover because both are expensive needs. But while I could not go back to the days of sitting in an enclosed space thick with drifting, languorous sheets of smoke from other people's cigarettes, I do not regard smokers as the devil incarnate as some seem to.

As the government considers a new bill on toughening up laws on smoking in public spaces to align with the European Union's Tobacco Products Directive, I can spare a thought for what it must be like to have your social life forever fragmented by negotiating the right to go somewhere with ashtrays on the tables. It isn't much fun for the non-smokers either. I socialise with a few smokers and always feel a twinge of bereftness when, after half an hour or so of catching up, I notice one of my nicotine-lovers friend's hands creeping towards the pack of cigarettes on the table and register that it's a prelude to them abandoning us all for a bit while they go and satisfy their craving outside. "Come back!" I want to cry as I observe them smoking reflectively by themselves at the entranceway – "I miss you!"

Now amongst other stipulations being tabled is a ban on smoking in public buildings and open-air spaces. This includes electronic cigarettes. Where is it all going to end?

The anti-smoking laws in Cyprus have always muddled me up. I remember when they first round came in, back in 2010, there was a provision by which a restaurant or bar owner could still accommodate smokers by creating an enclosed space that yet wasn't enclosed and from then on, the law got so convoluted and nonsensical that trying to interpret it was enough to make someone from Mensa feel like a thicko.

In any case, it had little impact. I remember one smoking friend taking me on a special nicotine mini-tour of a handful of places he knew in Paphos where you could puff away unrestricted. In one, we even bumped into a man who was mayor of Paphos at the time whose name I can't say without wanting to spit (he was ousted for corruption). So much for the authorities keeping an eye on law and order.

I have sympathy with The Pancyprian Association of Leisure Centre Owners (PASIKA) who are objecting to the new round of proposed laws. As I write this on my balcony, garbed in shorts and a tank-top, our fellow Europeans in France and the UK are now wearing boots and gloves. But Cyprus is an open-air society for the better part of the year and outdoor smoking anywhere is OK by me, a non-smoker.

Legislators, when fine-tuning the next round of laws on where smokers can and cannot light up, look around you, clock the local non-Brusselian climate and be reasonable.

October 2016

Save our souls

Likely there's someone out there who knows more about this than me but isn't there a belief in some cultures that if you take someone's photograph, you steal their soul? It's one of these urban myths that I've always known but whence it comes I'm not sure. I know that it's something about mirrors being a portal between this world and another realm. Because cameras rely on reflection to capture images, there was some sort of wariness that the soul of anyone who had a camera pointed at them would be compromised in some way. When I thought about this at all, it was always something that intrigued my mind but went no further. Until the advent of Facebook that is.

After a few days of being out and about at this and that event and having one too many photographers sidling up snapping me and whomever I'm with, doing whatever mundane things we're doing, I'm beginning to understand this business of associating the flash of a camera with the feeling of having your soul nicked.

Before Facebook and Co., you'd go out to something and, yes, there'd probably be a photographer doing their thing while you were drinking your wine or buying your raffle ticket or, I don't know, chewing the fat with someone. I never used to give it any thought. If I did, it would be a vague comfortable knowledge that perhaps one photo of the VIPS would end up on an obscure page of a website, so I could safely assume I would not be there. Even better, the best shot of a slew would maybe end up in a company newsletter. And that would be that.

Not so anymore. Now you feel you always have to sit up straight, not put your arm around someone in fun, only take a sip of wine when you're sure there isn't an intrusive camera lens pointing at your face and - worst of all - you always have to have a smile on your face. My cheek muscles fair ache after an evening out.

You can barely go anywhere nowadays without an uncomfortable feeling that your image might end up in cyber space in the name of someone posting every ruddy photograph from their get-together on social media to make it look like it was the happening of the year. It's another one of these intrusive things about modern life along with people texting while you're conversing with them or loudly yapping on their mobile in public places.

Leave your customers/ clients/ passers-by etc. alone, I want to tell event organisers. At least ask them if they object to being snapped so they can say no if it will allow them to enjoy the evening.

If you see photos of a Paphos event on social media featuring someone with her hands over her face – that was me. If you see a shot of the ceiling or sky because the photographer was knocked down – that was also me.

Date unknown

November

Where the streets have no name

It has occurred to me, not for the first time, how bizarre but liberating it is that I don't know the name of the street I live on. It could be March 25th or April 1st Street. I'm not really sure. I've never needed to know. My post gets sent to a PO box and, if I have to direct someone to my house, I tell them it's behind CYTA. Of all the streets I walk along in Paphos, I know the names of about three. I think.

If I try to explain to friends and family visiting from countries afar that everything goes on landmarks here, they don't get it. Sometimes, I don't get it.

When I lived in London, I would never leave the house without my dog-eared A-Z, a cartographical bible that pinned down everything from Trafalgar Square to any hokey-pokey little cul-de-sac somewhere in, say, Palmers Green.

Oh, I always knew where I was going in London and I certainly had no doubt about where I lived.

In contrast, here in Paphos, half the time when I'm setting out somewhere new, I only have the vaguest idea of where I am heading. But I am absolutely confident that I will find it and I always do. I just pull over and get directions – jam-packed with landmarks.

Just how accustomed I have become to this luxuriously lax way of getting around was brought to a head when I met my older sister in England for what was meant to be a nice family get together. It's worth noting that my sister lives in Toronto where they're used to the grid layout.

We were conferring about how to get to a famous stone circle. I knew it was "up that hill somewhere and why don't we just head in that direction and ask someone on the way" whereas she insisted that "someone get off their butts and find a tourist office, so we can grab a map and know where we're going!"

I didn't think this was necessary. In a fit of sibling paranoia, convinced I was trying to wind her up, she flung an open bag of crisps in my face.

Anyway, rumour has it that Sat Nav is coming to Cyprus soon. I can hardly wait.

"Turn right at the church with the broken window and go straight past where the old hospital used to be. Stop in front of the place that sells charcoal….".

November 2008

Ouzo mountains

At about five o'clock each day, when I am in the busiest throes of all my reporting jobs, I allow myself to switch off by gazing at something that looks like a light blue mountain range. Above it is a ribbon of pale yellow which blends into icy pink and blue. I absorb this replenishing sight for a few minutes then turn back to the computer and carry on pounding out words about statistics, police reports, tourism initiates, restaurants and the protection of Halloumi cheese.

When, after a while the words begin to stumble over one another, I sit back and take another look at the 'mountain range' which is now mauve and appears to have a rich golden spotlight emanating from somewhere inexplicable beyond. The light illuminates streaks of turquoise and peach and cream blue and I find myself wishing it was something I could turn into liquid and drink. I just know it would be more refreshing than a cold shot of ouzo and as revitalising as Viennese coffee. Then, I tell myself to get my imagination in check, so I can churn out more words about the Cyprus industrial turnover, spa treatments, dangerous roads, blood banks, sewerage and white wallabies at the local zoo.

At about quarter to six, when I sneak another look, what I am looking at has turned into a painter's blend of rust, indigo and magenta, and I swear that if someone could make me a dress with that exact subtle combination of colours, I would pay €1000 for it. Then I watch, hypnotised, as it sinks suddenly into dazzling black.

I am talking, of course, about the Paphos sky in autumn.

In all the countries I have lived in, I don't think I have seen anything as truly breath-taking as the autumn Cyprus western coast firmament when the sun is setting. The view I have of the sky from my desk is like a wide cinema screen for which I have a season's pass.

Who needs lava lamps, water features or a glass of ouzo when they have the Paphos sky to seduce them every afternoon?

November 2009

Who is watching who?

I grew up on a Neighbourhood Watch street and I am not warped, traumatised, a tittle-tattle nor a neurotic net curtain twitcher because of it. However by the way certain factions of Peyia Municipality are reacting to this successful global neighbourhood security programme, you would think that its introduction there is going to see the village turned into a blood bath.

The purpose of any Neighbourhood Watch scheme is to formally round up the help of residents to fight crime (commonly break-ins and burglaries) through them acting as 'eyes-and-ears' support for police. Information on suspicious activities or people is reported to area coordinators who monitor it and hand it over to police for investigation, if they see fit.

Last week, the municipality very publicly declared that it would not endorse this scheme's local set up early next year. What this means is that it won't assist financially or administratively. Why not? Because it is "concerned about resident safety and thinks trained professionals should deal with crime" it says.

I can't in a million years understand why anyone would regard Neighbourhood Watch as being dangerous to the public. On my childhood street in a Toronto suburb, there were no gun fights between residents and criminals. Our family did not position ourselves at the living room window after dinner and, Nazi Youth-style, surreptitiously take notes about goings-on outside for report to some Gestapo-like figure. Nobody was shot dead and nobody's car was blown up. In fact, the only memory I have of Neighbourhood Watch was a sign saying 'This is a Neighbourhood Watch Community' positioned at the entrance to the road - a warning to would-be crooks that this, perhaps, was not the best place to attempt a break-in.

I would have sympathy for the 'concerns' of Peyia Municipality Council if they hadn't been privy to the details of the scheme. But the Cyprus Chief of Police himself has been to Peyia along with a bevy of top officers to outline how it all works. They have met with Peyia Municipality about it and only a couple of months ago, the mayor applauded and expressed his support for Neighbourhood Watch at its official inception meeting which was thronged with hundreds of residents who are concerned about rising crime. The municipality stance U-turn is something of a mystery and, in a district where break-ins are even worse than we are told, the outright rejection of the scheme strikes me as somewhat irresponsible not to say disappointing.

I mean the police, the community police and a dedicated group of largely retired residents are all cooperating to clamp down on crime, but Peyia Municipality is refusing to get its finger out? Yes, I know that the political bods there keep saying they are demanding more police. But when are they arriving?

November 2010

Carpe Diem

How amusing was this week's warning from The Central Bank of Cyprus on the use of Bitcoin, the virtual currency which was launched in 2009?

"Extremely dangerous" were the precise words the bank used to describe virtual money in general as it is "not monitored by any authority, thus operating without control."

And using a commercial bank isn't extremely dangerous? Try telling anyone in Cyprus that. Has the banking sector in Cyprus got such a short memory that the date March 16 this year, when everyone's deposits were frozen while Europe, and the island's financial and political leaders made ready to skim a chunk off all of them to save the island's butt, has been forgotten?

Ooops – sorry. My mistake. It is possible that not everyone was affected by this. Apparently, some people conveniently executed transactions beforehand and got their money out of the country. Wasn't this being investigated once upon a time?

And all this from a financial system that does 'operate with control'.

What the Central Bank didn't say was that at the end of August 2013, the value of all Bitcoins in circulation exceeded US$ 1.5 billion with millions of dollars' worth of Bitcoin exchanged daily. I guess that means quite a few people are happy to use it.

In case anyone doesn't know what Bitcoin is, this is from its website: "Bitcoin uses peer-to-peer technology to operate with no central authority or banks; managing transactions and the issuing of Bitcoin is carried out collectively by the network. Bitcoin is open-source; its design is public, nobody owns or controls Bitcoin and everyone can take part. Through many of its unique properties, Bitcoin allows exciting uses that could not be covered by any previous payment system."

It is simply another currency. It is simply another way of performing transactions.

Bitcoin has been widely associated, wrongly or rightly with the black market – a point which is often highlighted by its critics. So, cash and credit cards are squeaky clean?

Anyway, the black market would be flooded by salt if that was still a currency. In other words, it would be flooded by anything that was a means of commercial transaction. Jeans, lipsticks and nylon stockings have all been means of 'trading' too haven't they? So, what does that say about them? That I'm wearing illegal currency?

The University of Nicosia caused a ripple beyond these shores by accepting Bitcoin for tuition fees last month. It claims it is the first university in the world to do so. I think this is pretty gutsy and say good luck to it.

There have always been alternative currencies. It's understandable that people want to explore complementary ways of conducting transactions to conservative methods – especially when they lose their jobs or have their salaries cut and no longer have traditional currency at their fingertips. Especially when they have to keep eating. This is the ugly situation in Cyprus these days.

Who is the Central Bank of Cyprus to spout off about what currency people should touch or not?

Instead of slamming anything which isn't a euro-coin or note, the financial sector should be holding forums on alternative currencies in order to provide proper and rounded advice on the options and how they can be used in parallel with fiat currency.

November 2013

Good news but for how long?

I saw a strange sight today. A young man was riding along on his moped with a helmet on his head. To add to the peculiarity, he was coasting along at a legal speed and was paying attention to the cars around him rather than weaving in and out of them as though he owned the road.

Anyone who lives in Cyprus will know that this doesn't happen very often. It is reflective of some good news at last on the traffic front. The Communications Ministry announced a drop in road fatalities in 2012 by 9% on 2011. Apparently, Cyprus recorded one of the top decreases in the EU which was welcome news after a horrific rise in road deaths in 2011.

It's no surprise that the majority of drivers killed on the road are under the age of 25 and are not wearing a seatbelt or a helmet. I think anyone could have told the government that without even looking at the facts and figures. In my experience in Paphos, the careless and reckless drivers are nearly always young men. If they are in a car they are speeding. If they are on a moped, they don't have a helmet.

The reduction in road deaths is positive but 9% is a low figure. And while the reasons for death on the road are largely put down to not wearing a seatbelt or a helmet, when the police do hit the roads in one of their campaigns, the top offences they clamp down on are speeding and drunk driving. They also stick to busy roads. But the serious fatalities usually happen on village roads.

The Ministry said that more concerted effort is needed by the state, municipalities, NGO's and the private sector to address road deaths. I agree. They need to get even tougher with the boy racers. It's bad enough that these careless drivers put their own lives at risk. They also put the lives of others in jeopardy as well.

November 2013

Regroup and rethink

So, the community garden in Yeroskipou has not taken off because not one of the 85 impoverished families who could use plots to grow their own food is interested. It is shocking that not a single person has shown any enthusiasm. The land has been donated. Yeroskipou Municipality will foot the bill for irrigation. All that's needed is some elbow grease to get the whole thing off the ground. Reasons, such as not having the time and having problems to deal with, are some given for a lack of eagerness to get involved.

It is a disappointment, but you can't help wondering why the plans have so far fallen on stony ground (if you'll excuse the pun). Similar schemes in the UK, for instance, are pretty successful. But maybe they aren't portrayed in such dismal terms. In short, could it be the way the project has been described?

Maybe it is a lost in translation matter but whenever I have spoken to the authorities about the project, they have described it as 'a vegetable garden for poor people'. Does anyone agree with me that this sounds awful? Even if you are broke and partly living on handouts, you still have your dignity. This sense that because someone is struggling money-wise, they should be grateful to do anything to put food on the table (in this case literally growing their own) has an ever so slight whiff of the workhouse about it. Perhaps this is what is unappealing.

Of course, there is no harm in expanding the catchment area of the scheme to include anyone in the region who is suffering a financial plight right now. Or maybe invite people who want to get involved but who don't need the fruits of their labour. Or how about a combination of volunteers who have an interest in learning the skills and some members of the families and individuals it is supposed to help?

Food grown in the plots could be gathered and distributed like any other donated goods. Who cares who grows it? Who cares who puts the work in? Who cares if the families who aren't interested in cultivating the plots still end up getting donations of food grown there? Does it matter? The main thing is that it is being done. If these 85 families are losing out on learning a useful skill (and it is a useful skill), well that's their loss quite frankly.

I can think of several good gardeners who don't need the charity of the food but could be interested in getting involved. How about widening the scope? The communal vegetable garden is an idea with potential but perhaps it needs to be rethought.

November 2013

Use your voice

I remember when there was a great deal of protest activity about the withholding of title deeds some years ago. This was before developers got wise to the fact that people investing huge sums of money into property, perhaps even their life savings, without any certificate confirming they were the legal owners of the property, was not the best publicity. It was also before the 2013 banking crisis which was a watershed of sorts for adjustments in all kinds of irregular conduct. Today, I am always amused when I read adverts issued by various developers where they feel it is important to let everyone know they have released 'X' number of title deeds. Well, at least their marketing departments know what's what.

Why am I harking back to title deeds? One uncomfortable image that stuck in my mind from that time is that of sizeable groups of British expats, mostly pensioners, tanned and looking like they would be more in place at dinner with friends or at a tribute act at one of the pubs on Tombs of the Kings Road, brandishing placards on sticks, bearing satirical or outright insulting messages to the effect of demanding their title deeds.

All I could think of as I surveyed these different groups was doubting for an instant that a single one of them had signed up to become placard holders in their retirement years in Cyprus where the "sun shines for 325 days of the year" and "everyone speaks English" and "driving is on the left".

My point is, that the end of next week is the final deadline for EU expats to register to vote in the December local elections. While I understand that not everybody is or wants to be politically active, or even cares that much about what may be going on at their local community council or municipality, there is still a good reason to make the effort to register to vote. For certain services that make life that little bit easier, like the establishment of a post office or an ambulance presence, the government assesses legitimacy of a community's needs based on the number of voters who are registered there.

Registration is free, and no knowledge of Greek is necessary. The process is straightforward, with voting application forms available at all District Offices and Citizen Advice Bureaus. You may only want to add your name to the list and increase the voting body figure, or you may, like the protestors described above, one day find you need to have a voice in local affairs.

November 2016

What lurks around the corner

There is nothing like being hit on by a man old enough to be your great grand-dad to make your skin crawl and your stomach lurch and when this happens in a public space, well, it's just degrading.

On enough occasions over the past six months or so, for it to be a noticeable occurrence, I have been on the receiving end of the most disgusting behaviour from octogenarian curb crawlers who, judging from their persistence, seem to misread a woman's act of turning her head in the opposite direction and pretending she can't hear their lecherous honking as a sign of interest.

I have found that this unwanted attention always happens on a weekend in the early afternoon. Maybe, in spite of all the years I have been in Cyprus, there is something I don't know. Maybe, if you are a woman, you aren't meant to walk by yourself from A to B in broad daylight on a Saturday or Sunday.

When I write about the aforementioned honking, I mean honking. Every lady is used to the odd honk of – well, I don't know if it's admiration or degradation, but never mind – from a passing car. But I'm talking driving along beside you, honking, doing a U-turn and honking at you from the other side of the street and then parking up ahead with the engine idling, waiting for you to pass so they can honk some more.

All the while you have to try to hold your chin up, pretend you don't notice and feel self-conscious and ridiculous. I would like to say that it's only me this has happened to, but it isn't. A couple of my friends have had the same unsavoury experiences, and have, like me, noticed they've come about over the last few months. Elderly men with bellies sagging over their seatbelts shamelessly take it into their heads to trail them as they try to walk along, minding their own business. Honk, honk! Ela!

In your dreams, grandpa! Go back home to your wife and grandkids. That's where you belong, not on the streets hassling women who are neither dressed provocatively, nor behaving in any suggestive manner, and who haven't demonstrated the slightest bit of interest in your orchestrations.

November 2016

A time to remember

This Sunday there will be two services in Paphos District marking Remembrance Day, held November 11. The day has been held since the end of the First World War in order to honour members of the Entente armed forces who died in the line of duty during that conflict and the Commonwealth military who served in World War Two. It is also held for contemporary conflicts.

I tend to think of Remembrance Day a little differently. For me, it's a day when I spare a thought for anybody (not solely members of the military) who has died or had their life damaged by warfare. In the last century alone, the bloodiest in history if I am not incorrect, how many civilians got up one day to get on with mundane tasks and didn't live to see another dawn because their homes were bombed, or they got caught in the crossfire of a battle. How many people are still experiencing this today?

Cyprus is a place that knows very well what ugly military conflict means. It has affected several generations over the 42 years since the Turkish invasion, occupation and division of the island. How easy it is to nearly forget, with the 320-plus days of sunshine a year that the tourist authorities tout, a welcoming azure sea and a pace of life that has not yet been corporatised, that, on the same island, there are the remains of people who went missing in 1974, today reduced to collections of bones, labelled, returned to loved ones and prepared for burial. That there is a scar-like line crossing and dividing the island into two zones, with pain and grief on both sides. That there are vandalised churches north of the line and empty mosques south. That there are homes which were left and never returned to. None of this has been put to rest.

Then there are the animals. At long last in 2004 in the UK, they created a war memorial in Hyde Park for all of the animals that have been dragged, no doubt terrified, into human war zones and slaughtered there. Mules, horses and elephants have been drafted to carry supplies and soldiers, carrier pigeons enlisted to deliver messages and dogs trained to lay underground communication cables. Australia and Canada have also built war memorials for animals and I am sure there are more scattered around the world that I am not aware of. Perhaps the words on the Hyde Park memorial put it most succinctly and ironically: "they had no choice".

I'm grateful to the people who organise the Remembrance Day services in Cyprus, although they bring up sombre reflections on beautiful, balmy autumn days.

November 2017

Clean up the roads

It looks like some progress is being made on the animal welfare front although it's not perhaps something to be jubilant about but rather simply grateful. I'm writing about the announcement of The Public Works Department agreement to a two-month pilot when a private company will pick up and dispose of the island's road kill.

I'm especially pleased to hear this because it means I won't have to do it myself anymore. Yes – if the carcass is more or less still in one piece, I'm one of those weird people who will pull over, don a pair of gloves, remove poor run-down animals, usually cats, from the middle of the street and place them at the side of the road for pick up by the rubbish authorities. If it's a regular route, the alternative is seeing the said carcass in increasing stages of dismemberment and flattening as traffic travels over it day and night. This puts me in a bad mood for all sorts of reasons. I don't think anything should end up like this.

But forget about mere residents like me. I'm surprised it's taken so long for the authorities to do anything about road kill for how off-putting it is for tourists alone. I've got used to looking out of the car or bus window and seeing dogs and cats lying dead at the roadside, but I didn't always used to be like this. When I first came to Cyprus, it upset me no end. Of course, I have toughened up since then, but it isn't difficult for me to imagine what it's like for fresh pairs of eyes. In short, it looks like nobody anywhere gives a damn. It looks putrid on both a basic cleanliness level and an ethical one.

Sadly, it's a sign of a perennial problem; the stray cat and dog over-population on the island. The island's Environment Commissioner, the Veterinary Services, the Pancyprian Coordinating Committee for Animal Welfare and District Councils have recently kick-started discussions on setting up a neutering programme to control the stray population. Stick to your guns on this one government. It's one of the kindest things anyone can do for strays.

Date Unknown

December

May old frocks be forgot

Feminine imagination is a powerful thing and the advertising teams behind perfume, make-up and shoes know it. They tap into that female instinct for glamour and mystery and get us to part with our cash for things we end up wearing or using once. But, still, I think feminine imagination makes life more fun. I only wish I could turn it off sometimes. Like now - when I am cleaning out my wardrobe as part of my New Year's resolutions.

I have resolved to give to charity every piece of clothing that I haven't worn within the last year.

I pluck out and consider an elegant grey dress dating from the 1930s that I have had for years but not worn since I don't know when. I ruthlessly fling it on the 'charity' pile but, no, something objects. "Come on," says my Feminine Imagination. "That dress is so Paris and Anaïs Nin and the French literary scene." Illogically, back into the closet it goes.

What's next? Uh-oh. A yellow, leather minidress I plan to start wearing just as soon as I have dyed it orange – something I have been meaning to do for two years. "You will never get around to it," I tell myself. "Put it on the pile. Quickly! Do it!" The dress is just about to end up on the 'charity pile' when my Feminine Imagination pipes up. "But I like it," it says through a pout, and the dress is returned to the closet.

As I sort through a pile of gym T-shirts my Feminine Imagination, thankfully, remains silent, but when I reach for a luxuriant blue velvet jacket that I haven't put on for three years, I brace myself. I fold it up and place it on the pile and am about to turn to a stack of scarves when a voice tells me: "But it is so Arabian Nights. You feel so exotic when you wear it." It's my Feminine Imagination sticking its oar in again. "Exactly – when I wear it!" I retort forcefully, "which hasn't been for ages." The jacket stays on the pile.

This goes on for two hours. Coats, blouses, skirts, belts, jewellery and shoes all undergo the battle of wills between my practical self and my Feminine Imagination. At the end of the tug of war, I have three piles of clothes which, hopefully, will make a few bob for one of the Paphos charity shops.

Next on my list of New Year's resolutions is sorting through my bookshelves, which are stuffed with unread books. This is going to be just as tough because, for this, I will have to grapple with my 'Intellectual Imagination'. I can already hear it: "Lucie. When you decide to take up quantum physics or to teach yourself Hungarian, you will kick yourself for throwing those books away…."

Wish me lots of luck.

December 2008

Say Merry Christmas while you still can

Not sure if there's going to be much of a 'Merry Christmas' anywhere this year.

I'm not referring to the grimness of the global economic collapse. I mean, literally, I don't think there is going to be a Merry Christmas this year. In fact, Cyprus might be one of the only places left on earth where there can be a Merry Christmas or 'Kala Christouyenna'.

In the UK, it seems that Big Brother has taken a dislike to the words 'Merry Christmas'. He thinks that phrases like 'Happy Holidays' and 'Winter Fest' are more politic.

In Canada and the US, you can practically go to jail for saying it. Why? Oh, someone, somewhere has decided that it might upset the non-Christian minorities, who I bet on the whole, couldn't care less what people say at Christmas – oops – Winter Fest.

What is in the psyches of Anglo-Saxon nations that impels them to give everything of their cultures away on a silver platter with accompanying cutlery and finger bowls?

These days, I live on an island where I baldly and routinely get called a foreigner. A neutral word in Greek, it's nearly a dirty word in English and makes me flinch every time I hear it – at the bank, at government offices, by my friends. I live in a country where, I don't think I can bear it if I have to remove one more dead cat from the road or take a scabby, ill, stray kitten to the vet to be put down. I live in a country where I have stopped taking for granted that anyone will stand up for my rights. Too many experiences to the contrary have knocked that on out of me.

But the longer I live in Cyprus, the more I appreciate it. I am grateful I live in a country where political correctness has not descended, and I can still say Merry Christmas without going to court.

Long may it last and, whatever it means to you, Merry Christmas.

December 2009

Magical journeys

If I am travelling back from Limassol, I usually drop off the motorway at Aphrodite's Rock and complete the last leg of the journey home along the old road. I wasn't prepared for how enchanted I would be by the roadside Christmas décor when I took this route a few nights ago.

First, I passed the entrance to Aphrodite Hills which was swathed with a myriad of blue lights. Dotted alongside the road were sparkling Christmas trees. For some time after that the road was inky. There weren't any other drivers about and I was travelling under a column of fir trees and all that was lit up were the reflective cats' eyes on the road. Then I saw a fog of light up ahead and understood that I was approaching a village. "I wonder what Christmas lights they'll have there," I thought to myself. As it turned out, a large star on top of a restaurant, illuminated bells hanging from the lamp posts and a lit-up banner bearing the message 'Kronia Bolla', meaning Happy Returns.

This carried on all the way back to Paphos. I would hit a stretch of black road with only the speed limit signs illuminated. Then I would suddenly find myself in one of the villages and would slow down to savour what was on offer; a string of lights strung haphazardly but earnestly around some bushes, a nativity scene, pretty clumps of shining blue and green and yellow Christmas trees and glittering doves hung across the street. Back on the black road a lone house would loom out of the darkness with a Christmas tree glowing in a window. I passed a palm tree wrapped tightly in little festive lights.

Next were the outskirts of Yeroskipou then the village square. Beautiful lights appearing to drip down the walls of the town hall and icicles in every shade of blue hung in intervals across the road. An elegant tree was speckled with lights. I decided to bypass my home in Yeroskipou and finish the journey properly at Paphos Town Hall Square where the Municipality have done a magnificent job on the surrounding Christmas décor. I especially liked the clusters of little reindeer which are composed of tiny lights.

Maybe, like me, you have passed Christmastime in all sorts of cities. Zurich is just breath-taking, dripping with lights. London has its traditional Norwegian spruce tree in Trafalgar Square, an annual gift from Norway to Britain for its help during WWII. Paris has its wonderful shop window displays.

But the simple, heartfelt and unexpected decorations of the villages in Paphos are always enough for me.

December 2010

Strange journeys

At Paphos airport, there were scores of Canadian soldiers leaving for their homes in Canada for Christmas. For at least four years now, the Canadian army has been using Paphos as a base for decompression after a tour of service in Afghanistan. The military personnel arrive fresh from the combat zone and stay in a Paphos hotel to 'acclimatise' before being reunited with their families and friends. At the airport, they were scattered around the café in their fatigues listlessly using their laptops or sleeping with their heads on folded arms.

I was going to Canada too – to Toronto, to visit my family for the holidays. As we commercial passengers were ferried by bus from the departure lounge to the plane, we passed an ugly, hulking, grey military aircraft with 'Canada' written on one side.

One soldier was not returning home via Paphos. His name was Steve Martin. He was a 24-year-old Corporal and had been killed in an explosion in Afghanistan one week before Christmas. He was going back to Canada and the festive season in a box.

I didn't know any of this at the time. I learnt about it while, a couple of days after arriving in Toronto, I was on my way to a shopping plaza for some groceries. To get to the shops I had to cross a bridge which spans one of the busiest highways in the world named the 401. As I walked with the minus-10 cold blistering my face and my breath hanging in the air, the climate struck me as vicious. I didn't know how anyone could function in it. So, I was surprised to see a substantial crowd congregated on the bridge as I approached. They were on the side of the overpass which was facing the multiple lanes of oncoming traffic and they were watching it expectantly. "What are they doing hanging around in this cold?" I asked myself as I started to cross the bridge. I soon found out.

The crowd consisted of off-duty fire, police and ambulance crews as well as passersby like me. Some of them were holding Canadian flags. One or two were weeping. Others were chatting. I asked someone what was happening, and they explained that they were waiting for a funeral convoy of a soldier who was killed in Afghanistan. Following standard procedures, the body had been flown to a military base outside the city to be received by family and was now making its way along a 10km stretch of the 401 into Toronto for delivery at the coroner's office.

Since 2002, whenever such a funeral convoy travels into the city, people gather in all-weather on each of the overpasses over the highway to show their solidarity with a family which has brutally lost a precious loved one. On the day I happened to be passing it was the journey of Corporal Steve Martin.

The convoy eventually approached. Traffic on either side instinctively slowed down as much as was possible. People waved from the bridge and someone waved back from a car. Then the convoy slipped beneath the underpass and carried on into the city.

The Canadian soldiers at Paphos airport were going home from a war zone, I was travelling home for the holiday season and Steve Martin from Quebec was going home covered in a Canadian flag.

So many strange journeys start in our part of the world.

December 2010

Question Time

If someone has something important to say and they can't say it in a maximum of one pithy minute, in my view, there is something wrong. I will be generous and, for politicians both incumbents and aspiring, will extend this time frame to eight minutes. In fact, I think it should become law that campaigning politicians cannot spend more than eight minutes presenting their successes, successes and more successes to the public. It should be enshrined in a new Article 31 of the UN Universal Declaration of Human Rights as a violation if they go one second over this time limit.

This is because the scores of three million-year long election campaign addresses for Sunday's local poll I have necessarily been subjected to over recent weeks violate Article 5 (no one shall be subjected to torture). Why torture? If the drip, drip, drip of nebulous litanies of how these political candidates have saved the world, are saving the world and are going to continue saving the world is not torture I don't know what is. I am surprised nobody has said they have found a cure for cancer amongst the promises to save the economy, feed all the stray animals and bring a better quality to life to all our children.

How many times in the last month have I come back from some love fest of a campaign address, switched on my computer to write a report and found myself staring into space with my hands poised frozen over my keyboard not knowing how to convert clouds of meaningless phrases into something that, hopefully, people want to read? How I have longed to hear someone admit that "we are in the s**t, this is how we got here, and this is how we can try to get out" and actually back up their claims with some credible plans which aren't composed of verbal candy floss.

This leads to my next criticism. I have lost count of the number of addresses I have been to for these elections but one thing they have all had in common, save one, is that there has not been adequate time for questions from the public. This is where the nit and grit is (by the way, if you are allowed to ask your question. I was fussily rapped on the knuckles by one address organiser for asking an 'irrelevant' question. Excuse me, but I am a reporter which means I have the privilege of asking what I damn well want).

Instead of hearing candidates being machine-gunned with merciless questions (which is what they deserve), I have heard polite silences or cowardly detracting grumbles within the crowd. Instead of seeing them being grilled, I have seen them being ego-massaged. In some places I have fully expected to see blood, torn-out hair and ripped clothing but instead heard too much polite applause and too many 'bravos' and 'hear, hears'. I put this down to a lack of time for questioning. Eight minutes address; two hours for questions next time round please. Possibly I have missed those events.

I have been astonished at what I have experienced. And for all the wrong reasons.

December 2011

15 years in Aphrodite's fishbowl

Nothing is too small

No need to go over the facts and figures yet again as, unless you have had a prolonged absence from the island, you will know that the economy is in a precarious state.

The rising number of empty shops for rent in Paphos are plain to see and increasing jobless numbers have been standard news fodder for a long while now. It is all indescribably depressing as there are, no doubt, countless tales of personal stress and misery behind all of the news reports.

If there is any good news in the scenario it is that the community is pulling together in order to help Paphos' growing segment of needy families and individuals in practical ways. It is very hard work for those involved. I have met a few of the volunteers who are gathering food and clothing for people with limited means. They say the efforts are relentless with the situation visibly worsening in the last six months. But they also say that they could not dream of turning a blind eye now.

Christmas, traditionally a time of generosity, is behind us once more but generosity is still desperately needed now and will continue to be needed next year. If you're having an end-of-year clean out of your wardrobe, you might want to siphon some items off for the clothing collection points. Likewise, all dried goods such as rice, pasta, cereals, pulses, canned goods and all kinds of baby food are top of the list for distribution to people who are struggling.

Off the top of my head I can think of two collection drives taking place right now. The first is at Paphos Town Hall; the second is taking place at Pavlina's, a clothing store. Both of the above drives are taking place for as long as there is a need. As one volunteer manning a collection point told me, even one tin of tomatoes helps. Nothing is too small.

December 2012

Stock up on sun screen

What has astounded me about the recent announcement that British pensioners residing in warmer climes will no longer be entitled to the Winter Fuel Allowance (WFA) as of the 2015 to 2016 winter, is not that it is on the road to being cut, but that half of the recipients have received it in the first place. That goes for pensioners both in the UK and abroad.

An issue that has been brewing for several years now with many Paphos ex-pat pensioners set to be affected, the British Government has said that it will axe the annual payment which works out at roughly €250 to €385 annually for each individual. The British Government has said triumphantly, as though it has done something very clever, that it has circumnavigated EU legislation which has dictated that all UK pensioners living abroad receive the allowance by introducing a "temperature test". What this means is that British pensioners in EU countries with a higher annual average temperature than that of the UK (5.6 C) can kiss the payment goodbye. In other words, according the British Government's genius 'means test', next winter pensioners in Cyprus, Portugal, France, Greece, Malta, and, the EU state with the largest number of British ex-pats Spain, will be living in countries which are too warm for a heating allowance. Better stock up on sun screen then.

The UK Daily Mail stated in a recent article on the subject that UK taxpayers pay just over €22 mln a year on the WFA to pensioners living abroad. Payments to Cyprus are about €1.8 mln while Spain sees around €11 mln.

It's quite embarrassing to see your own Government using a method for ascertaining if one qualifies for such a payment which is so rudimentary that a nursery school could improve on it. I mean what does 'average temperature' have to do with real life? What does the hottest most sweltering day in August in Cyprus have to do with the coldest breath-hanging-in-the-air day in January? If the government was going to do a means test based on an average temperature wouldn't it have made more sense to base it on that of the winter months?

But forget about ridiculous temperature means testing. From the off, qualification for the WFA should have been based on income. Have you seen the form you need to submit to get this payment? In a nutshell, as long as you were born before 1952 and aren't in prison, you're eligible.

Reminder: The WFA was brought in so that the elderly would not be at risk of dying of the cold through not being able to afford their heating bills.

I have no doubt that some local UK pensioners need every cent of this payment and use it in their heating budgets. I also have no doubt that others use it for beer money. I'm not criticising anyone for accepting the WFA; I'm angry that the British Government has been so lax with its handouts.

December 2014

Ancient relief

I find that life tends to crowd one out more and more as the years pass. I don't own a TV and am not a big film goer, so when I want to escape from it all, the way I do it is by reading or taking a walk. Another way I clock out for a bit is by wandering around some of the local ancient ruins.

I feel very fortunate that I live in a place where signs of other eras dot the landscape. It puts some of the jarring nature of day-to-day life in perspective when you can amble off into another century or millennium through the remains of temples and forts and artefacts.

It isn't just the ruins which are firmly on the tourist trail but those which aren't and, with the guidance of a book or someone who knows about them, you can explore. The Persian siege wall overlooking the Mediterranean and some nearly-forgotten tombs near Kouklia come to mind.

The fascinating discoveries of an archaeological expedition in Nea Paphos which were announced this week reminded me about the richness of history in Cyprus and this part of the world in general.

The Nea Paphos site is the location of the Greco-Roman House of Dionysus and the House of Orpheus. An excavation team from Poland have been making some fascinating discoveries! In the recent announcement, it said that they had unearthed a 1,500-year-old amulet with two sides bearing a palindrome inscription. This means the inscription reads the same way forwards as it does backwards. Descriptions in trade magazines say that one side of the amulet has several images imprinted on it including a bandaged mummy which could be the Egyptian god Osiris in a boat. It also has an image of the god of silence, Harpocrates, perched on a stool covering his mouth. The palindrome is written in Greek and refers to Iahweh, a god of the time. It translates as "Iahweh is the bearer of the secret name, the lion of Re secure in his shrine." The amulet also shows an image of a mythical creature with the head of a dog which is also covering its mouth with a paw, echoing Harpocrates.

Jagiellonian University professor Ewdoksia Papuci-Wladyka who led a Polish 2011 dig has commented on the amulet. She has said that an amulet was thought to protect owners. She also said that the object indicated the presence of both Christian and pagan traditions in Cyprus of the time, and that whoever made the object didn't have a full understanding of the mythical figures on its surface as they aren't depicted fully accurately. Oh, so human! Even all these literally awesome finds that archaeological teams come across in Cyprus show signs of fallibility.

This is one reason I find it so soothing to look at the ancient past. You just know that whatever troubles, big or small, there are in life today, time has seen it all before.

December 2014

Keeping in tune with tradition

While an utter novice on the epoque, I have a fascination with the Byzantine era. I like the art and the architecture, am intrigued by the history and was interested to learn recently that this historical period even has its own cuisine – the 'descendant' recipes of which are taught at a hospitality school in the capital.

This chapter in history strikes me, from my layman's view, as being very unique to this region, and also, though it may sound strange, unique in history itself. The Byzantine era seems to exist in a capsule – as if all the power struggles, intrigues, riches and artefacts you could ever want can be found then. Brutal, yes, but also rarefied is the word I would use.

The Christmas season and all of its musical offerings have reminded me of something I often forget – perhaps because, also rarefied, it was not connected to much else in my life at the time: I studied Byzantine music for two years at Paphos Bishopric.

Under the head cantor, a group of us would meet twice a week and learn the scales (or modes), going around the table one by one singing Ni, Pa, Vou, Gha, Dhi, Ke, Zo (similar to Do, Re, Mi). Gradually, we progressed to hymns and rehearsed for Easter and Christmas concerts performed for friends, family and some seasoned parishioners. I must have been an anomaly. I was the only out-of-towner and one of just two women, but I was accepted and welcomed into the introduction to this tradition, even though, after some probing, the others discovered I wasn't religious.

Over the two years, we worked with two, thick, hardcover books, crammed with the oriental-looking notation and archaic Greek of Byzantine music. I only scratched the surface of this complex musical system, but the two years were a special interlude. I found, and still find, the music to be quite solemn and meditative, like any sacred music, and would recommend any expat from Europe or further afield who wants to get a taste of a truly local Christmas cultural tradition to go to a concert of Byzantine music.

December 2016

Phone calls from other time zones

Today, December 18th, is my father's birthday. Normally I'd phone him but, this summer, he died suddenly and shockingly from an incurable cancer. It happened so swiftly that I didn't even get to Toronto, where he lived, in time to be with him for a few moments before he slipped away. As my plane approached Toronto airport the day after his death, my stomach was so tense I was in pain. At the same time, I felt a hollowness words will never be able to describe because he was precious to me and gone forever.

Not needing to make that phone call today is even harder than his funeral or receiving his cremation ashes were.

My story is not unusual. Paphos is full of people from all over Europe and beyond who get this kind of dreaded news all the time via a phone call from another time zone. How many times have I heard that this friend's husband has dropped dead of a heart attack in Sri Lanka or that an acquaintance's mother has passed away from an illness nobody even knew she had in Germany? Then long, uncivilised journeys have to be made to deal with the aftermath and you start wondering if all this globalisation and living in all corners of the world is worth it.

Ironically, on my return from Toronto after my father's death, I learned that a Greek-Cypriot Canadian who was sitting behind me was making a mirror image journey to mine. I knew all this because she was speaking loudly to her neighbour about how her mother, who had lived near Larnaca, had just died, also of cancer, and she was travelling to her funeral. The disease had been under control, she was saying, but it had suddenly come back, and her mother had died the day before. She was lucky to get a flight, she said.

As we neared Larnaca, she started speaking louder and louder and faster and faster. I think I had an inkling of what she was feeling. I wanted to get out of my seat, sit next to her, take her hand and let her spill everything out about the harrowing experience.

This time of year, you tend to look over the months and tot up who is still around and who has gone. And, you understand that, when it comes to the big things in life, we are all the same.

December 2009

Printed in Great Britain
by Amazon

14187481R00084